IN LOVE
AND DEATH

THE LOST NOTEBOOK

BERT
McCRACKEN

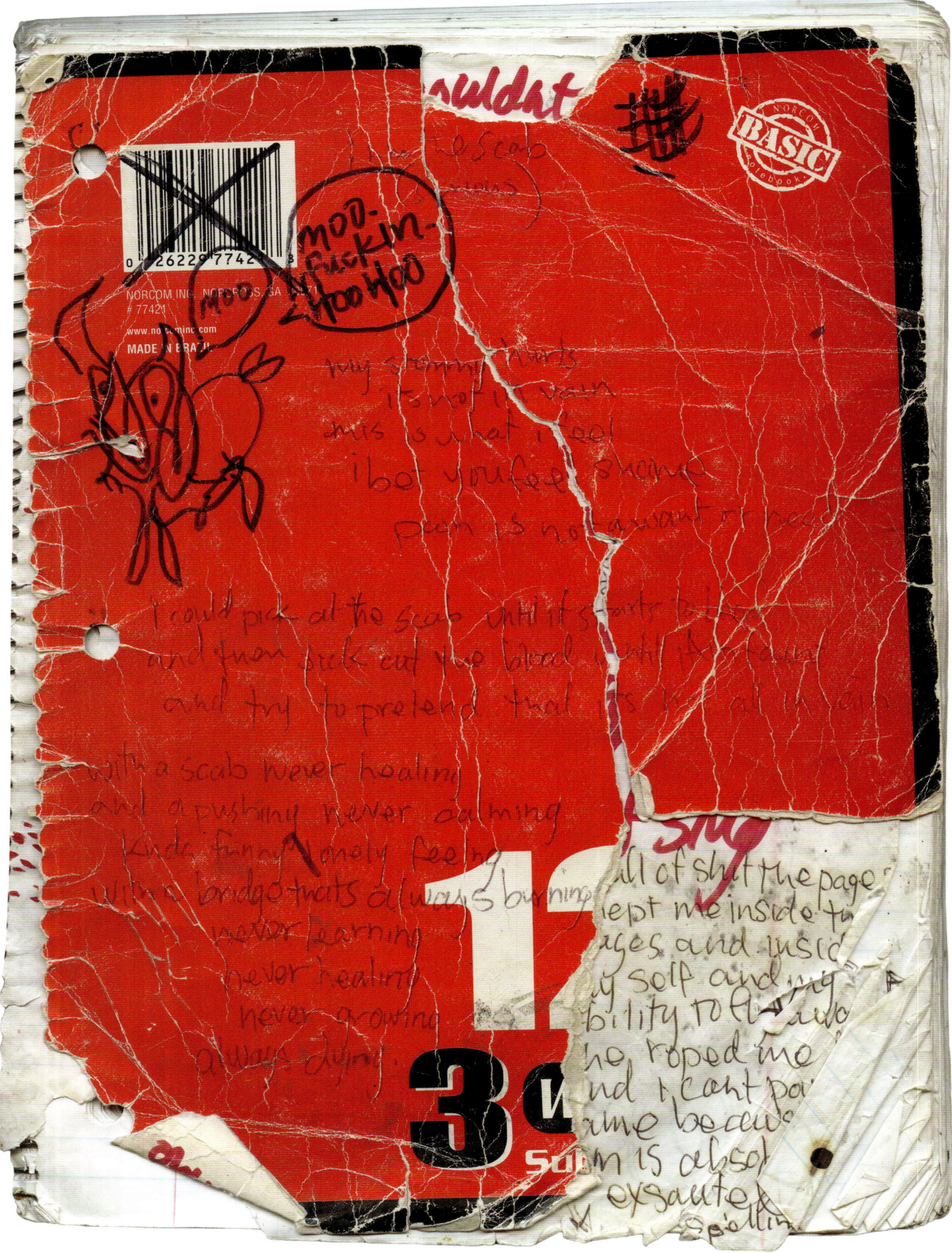

IN LOVE AND DEATH

THE LOST NOTEBOOK

BERT McCRACKEN

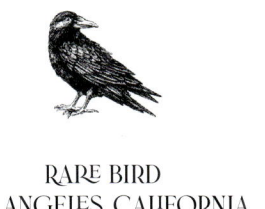

RARE BIRD
LOS ANGELES, CALIFORNIA

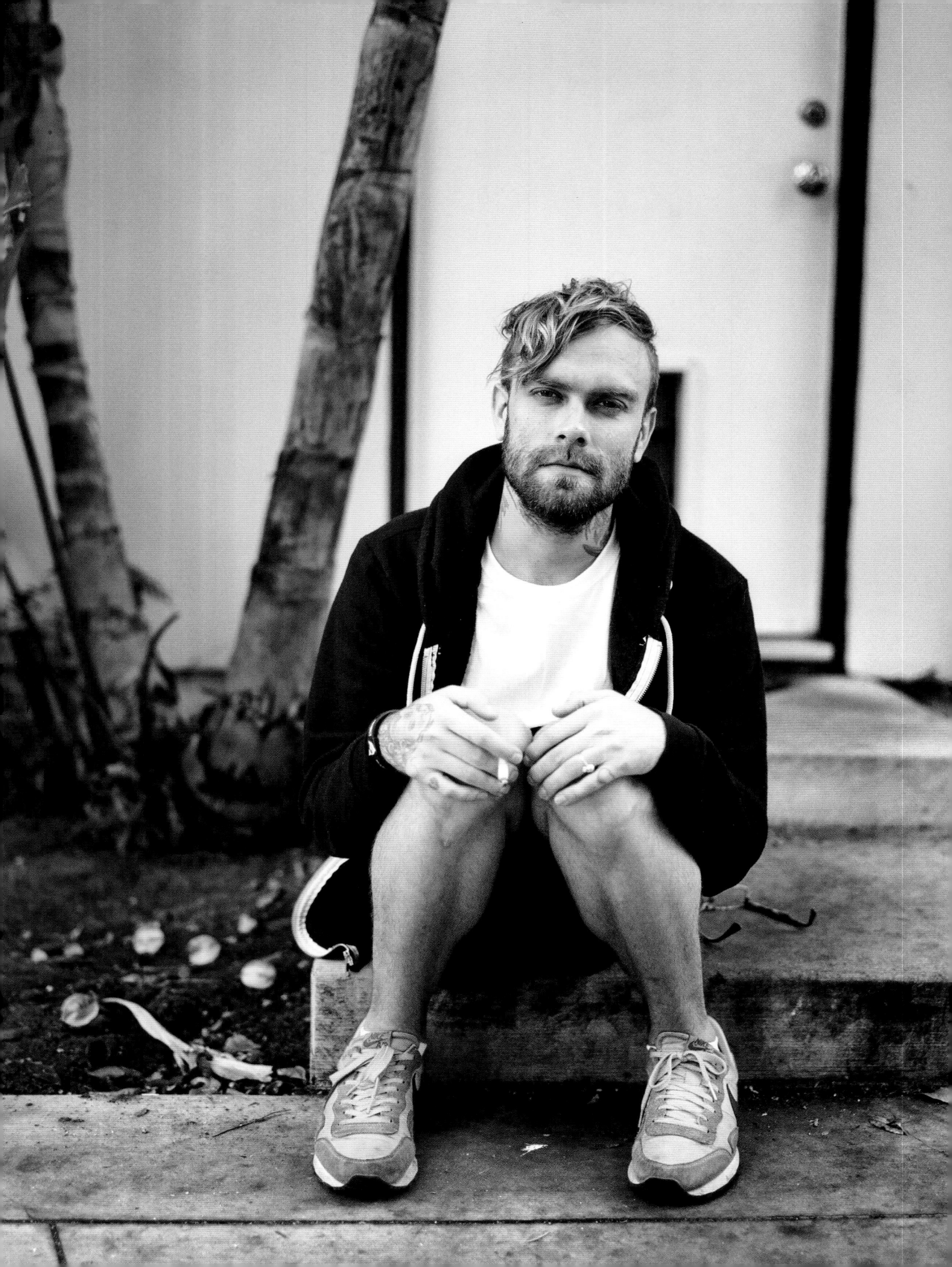

INTRODUCTION

This notebook contains my lyrics, poems, thoughts, sketches, and doodles from nearly twenty years ago. These scribblings were the origin point for everything I expressed throughout 2004's *In Love and Death*. When I learned that a stranger was trying to sell it online, I had to get it back into my possession.

I kept a big box of The Used memorabilia in my parents' basement in Utah. It's filled with letters from fans, little bracelets and necklaces, and assorted ephemera. One of my little brothers most likely showed the box to one of his friends and maybe gave the notebook away. He doesn't remember giving it away, and there's no reason I wouldn't believe him, but he wasn't much older than ten or eleven then.

The whole idea of writing your lyrics down in a physical journal is a lost art. People write on their laptops now, use the Notes app on their phones, or leave themselves a voice memo. Even from a technological standpoint, that wasn't available to me then—I'm not sure if we even had T-Mobile Sidekicks yet. I usually have a bunch of notebooks just kicking around. In 2003, I grabbed this one from one of my stacks.

I kept it around all the time. I doodled in there and made notes, both big and small. It wasn't so much a thought-out thing, really. I knew I would need lyrics eventually, so I'd jot down my ideas. Even if it was just like, "Fuck you, fuck you, fuck you." Anything can spur something at some point. It's good

to get the brain juices flowing, even when you don't know what to say, by just making yourself sit down and write.

I'd forgotten all about this notebook until it resurfaced online. *Holy shit*, I thought. *There's probably so much amazing shit inside.* I needed to see what's in there. I was desperate to get it back. Luckily, a friend of a friend knew the person selling the notebook and made a direct appeal for its safe return to me.

Getting it back into my hands and cracking it open for the first time in two decades brought back so many feelings. 2004 was a crazy, tough year for me. There was a lot of loss, first with my beloved chihuahua, followed by the death of my longtime girlfriend, Kate, from a drug overdose. My emotions spiked as I flipped through the pages. I couldn't believe what I'd written—how brave I was in my early twenties. It was also exciting to see some of the doodles and other random shit in there. So, I decided to share it.

The smell of grass takes me back to the Track and Field Day end-of-year celebrations at school. These writings evoke the same type of sense-based memories, like how music transports you back to when you first heard a song or discovered a new band. It's almost like I can taste or smell my life in 2003 and 2004.

This notebook is a time capsule. It's a snapshot of who I was and what I went through then. Who can remember things from so long ago in that much detail? But when I flip through this, I instantly recall those feelings, where I was mentally and emotionally, my attitude toward the world, and death in general.

The pages conjure vivid memories—even where I was and what I was up to when I wrote something down. Having a document of how the songs progressed from short poems to finished lyrics is a true gift.

Through the tragic situations that came about during the recording process, I turned to alcohol and drugs as a coping mechanism. Unfortunately, this pushed the band away, creating a gap I could not fill. My addiction has stood in the way of the things that I love, and I have no excuses. I will always be grateful to the boys for sticking by my side, even when I was unbearable to be around. *In Love and Death* happened because of all four of us. Quinn's riffs, Jepha's bass, Brandan's drums, and my vocals made this crazy, beautiful album come to life. I will forever look back at these times with both pain and joy for what we accomplished.

I love to read and always have, but I never thought I'd publish any book unless it were deep-dive, postmodern fiction where nothing happens, it doesn't go anywhere, and there's no ending. Getting this published was set in stone the minute I found the notebook and realized how much the lyrics and drawings encapsulated that time. I threw the idea out there, and when Rare Bird responded, I was overjoyed.

The older we get, the scarier it becomes to put ourselves out there. During the writing process for *In Love and Death*, whether I'd dig very deeply into my personal experiences on the album was never in question. I wasn't far from my drug-addicted path and even still meeting up with friends who were deeply in it.

Those are crazy memories, and it's simply unbelievable how far I've come.

The early work of many of my favorite authors seems so brave. However, we become less courageous about putting our whole selves into our writing. I look at this notebook and think, *Wow, that kid was fearless.* There was no second-guessing. To see what survived from all those words is magical.

Working with producer John Feldmann can be so fast-paced and crackling with energy that I'm mostly jotting down notes on my phone now. His process forces you to avoid overthinking, which is fantastic.

But I do still keep a notebook.

—Bert McCracken

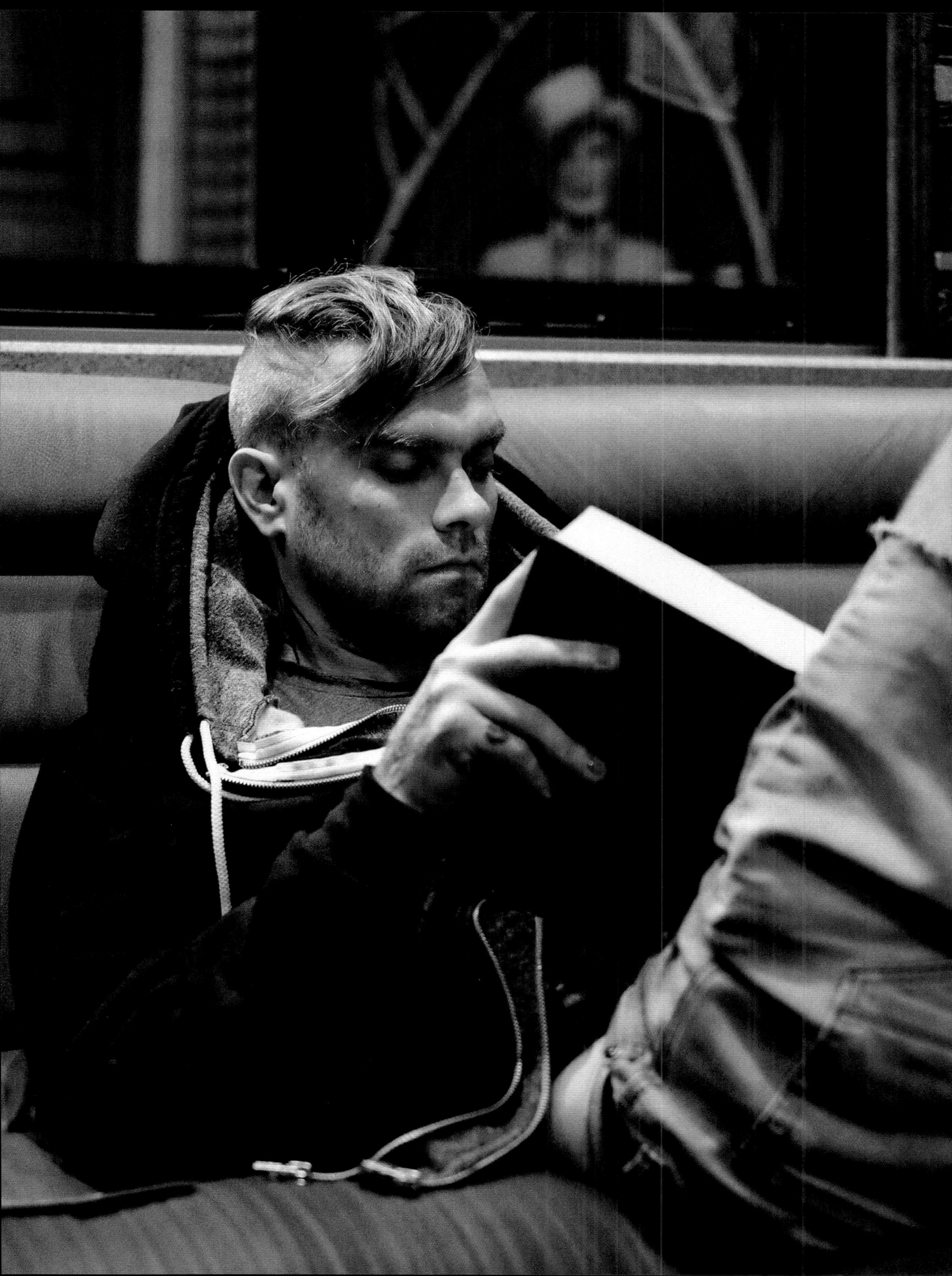

① (you're)
(skin)

this poisons my intoxication.
I broke the needle off in my vain.
picked the scab and picked the bleeding.
and assumed that it was all in vain.
a positive sign that's never healing.

Can't ask lit me in the face
a burning bridge is so unforgiving
poison more potent now like the flame.

↓

the fire dep. couldn't entrust the city.
didn't ought try to wash it clean
and what did you think was sober
put me out cause I'm on fucking fire
a positive sign that's never healing
regret but I kept this death
to for you is keep on dying.
the most that I can do for you let it sing.
its not a lie if you can let it sing.

② (was

(oh I might want to sing (maybe dying the might want to sing)
I wanna sing
or scream it
(if you feel like dying it)

let it bleed
and take the red 4 what
its worth and OH
watch the fire MAMA
fill your lungs w
smoke for the last time

in the quiet if
and it was
there is no ___
and it was fine,
a little small step

the fire dep couldnt drown i
didnt even try to wash it city
and what did you think that i was clean
~~with how i feel~~ im on. sober
~~cut me out cause~~ fucking fire
a positive scab thats never healing
a sigh of regret that i kept this
the most that i can do for you clean
is keep on lying
(mama rubber ~~cement~~ ~~your~~ you)HA
face to my)HA
dreams.)

Its not a lie
if you let it sing

* s right through me,*
night, no words to hold away.
eed some feelings
we need a cleansing
we need a burning
i cant forget how hot we got
in our awjness
so we still bit the bottle
and swalled the glass
and lived in the past
fell apart as they days
forget it forget
forgive me

full of shit the pages
kept me inside to
pages and inside
my self and
ability to fl
the roped in
and i cant pa
blame because
i am is absolutti
exsauted
spillin

9

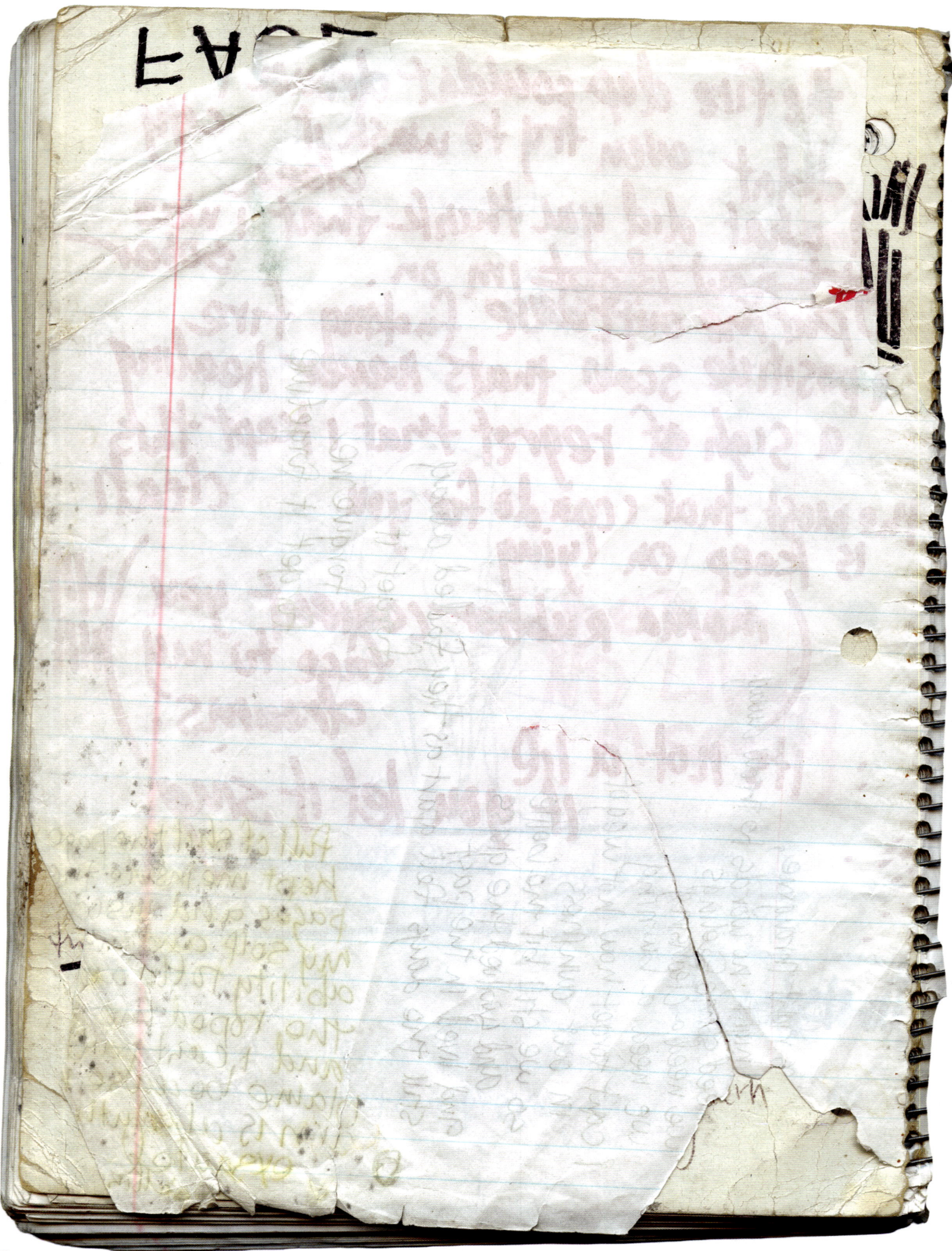

This was the journal that I wrote all the lyrics and the thoughts for *In Love and Death* from 2003 to 2004. This journal was left in a box in my parents' basement. It's just a box that I keep, a bunch of used paraphernalia, fan cards and whatnot. And a few years later my brother was showing off all this stuff to one of his friends and he just gave the journal away not knowing how important it was to me. His friend then gave it to another friend and it had been gone for years and I thought it was missing for good. Later, I saw the journal online for sale for $10,000.

What is in planning
and what's the connection
between her lies and his lies
and everything in between
Compromise
can't keep my head up
what you said make me sick
a super tiny little trumpe
you should clef. some

lay
lay down
feel faced with the
the little life expression
the little
one
and a vicious one
it was
super
duper

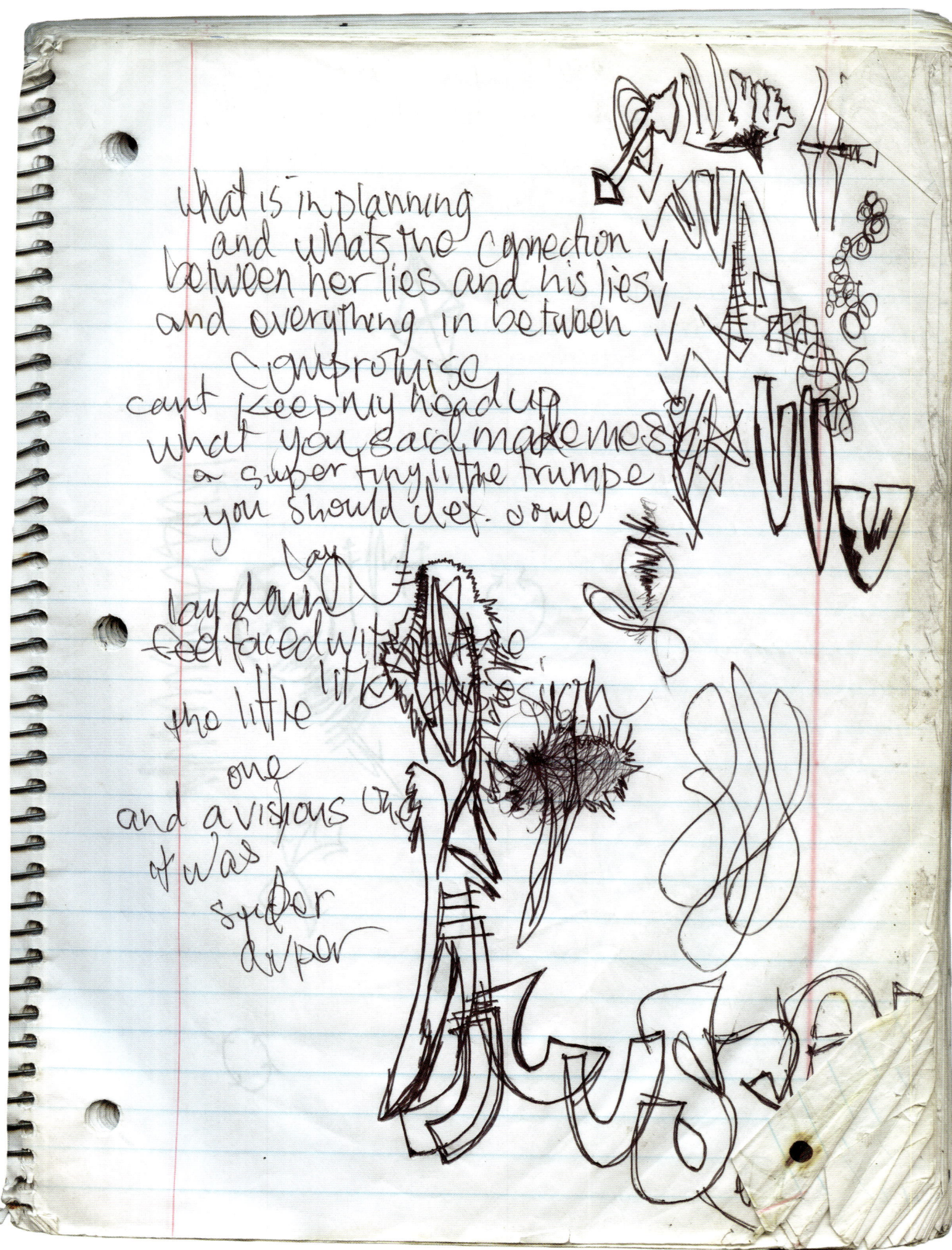

And so we tracked down
the original friend who had
contact with the journal,
and luckily I had a friend
outside of the whole circle
who knew the kid who was
selling it. We met with him
and nicely asked him to
please give it back
and he agreed.

maybe a cigarette all that I needed
sometimes feeling defeated
which I understand to be gone
although capable of climbing
I sat simply watching waiting breathing
in its purest
giving birth to firery sunsets
overbearing out of confidence
but somewhat certain in knowing
silence (check)
in being, watching, learning, loving

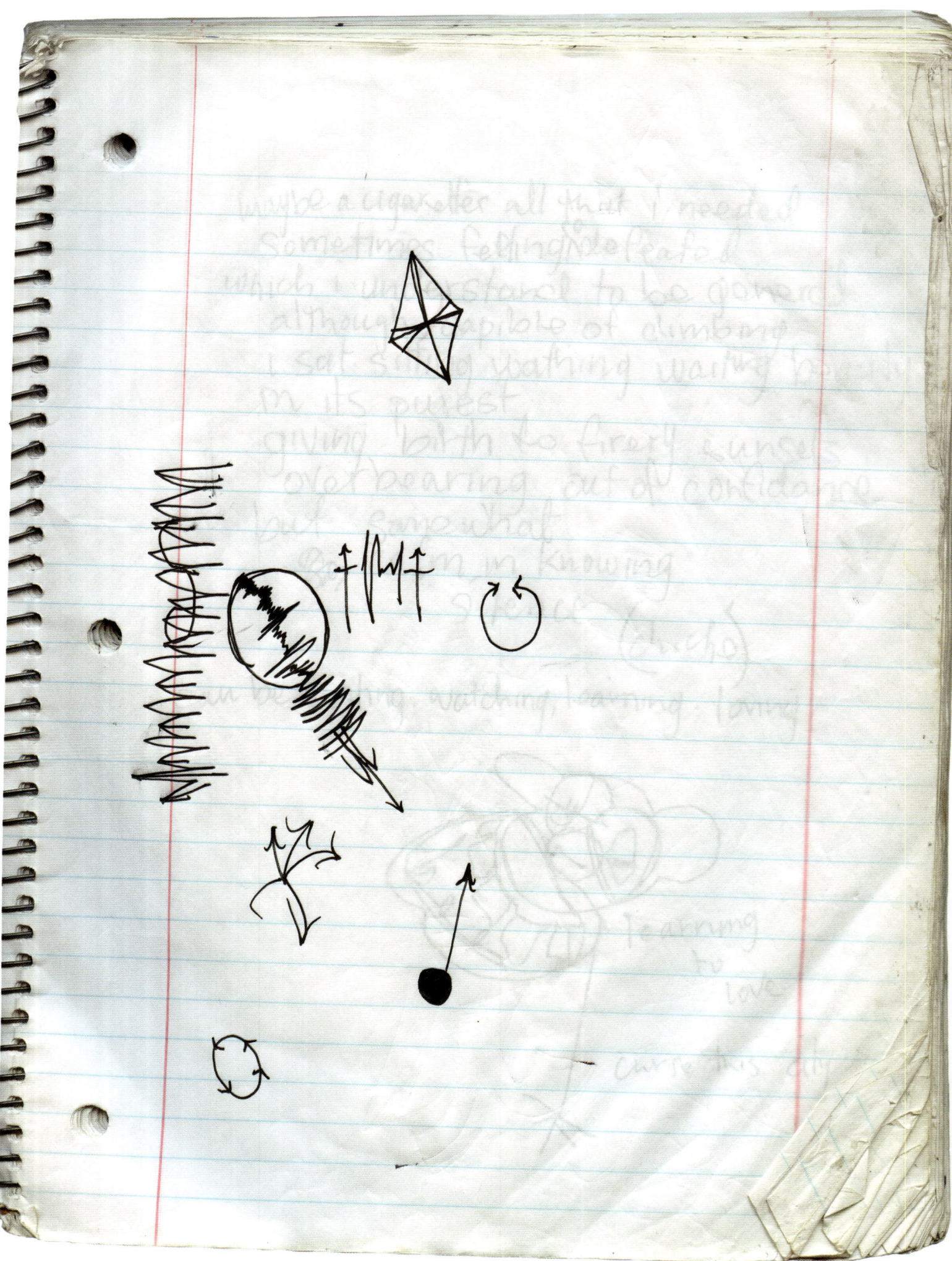

learning
to
love

cure this day

maybe a cigarette all that i needed
sometimes felling so defeated
which i understand to be goneral
although capible of climbing
i sat sitting wathing waiting beauty
in its purest
giving birth to firery sunsets
overbearing out of confidance
but somewhat
calm in knowing
silence
(chicho)

can be waiting. watching. learning. loving.

learning
to
love

curse this city

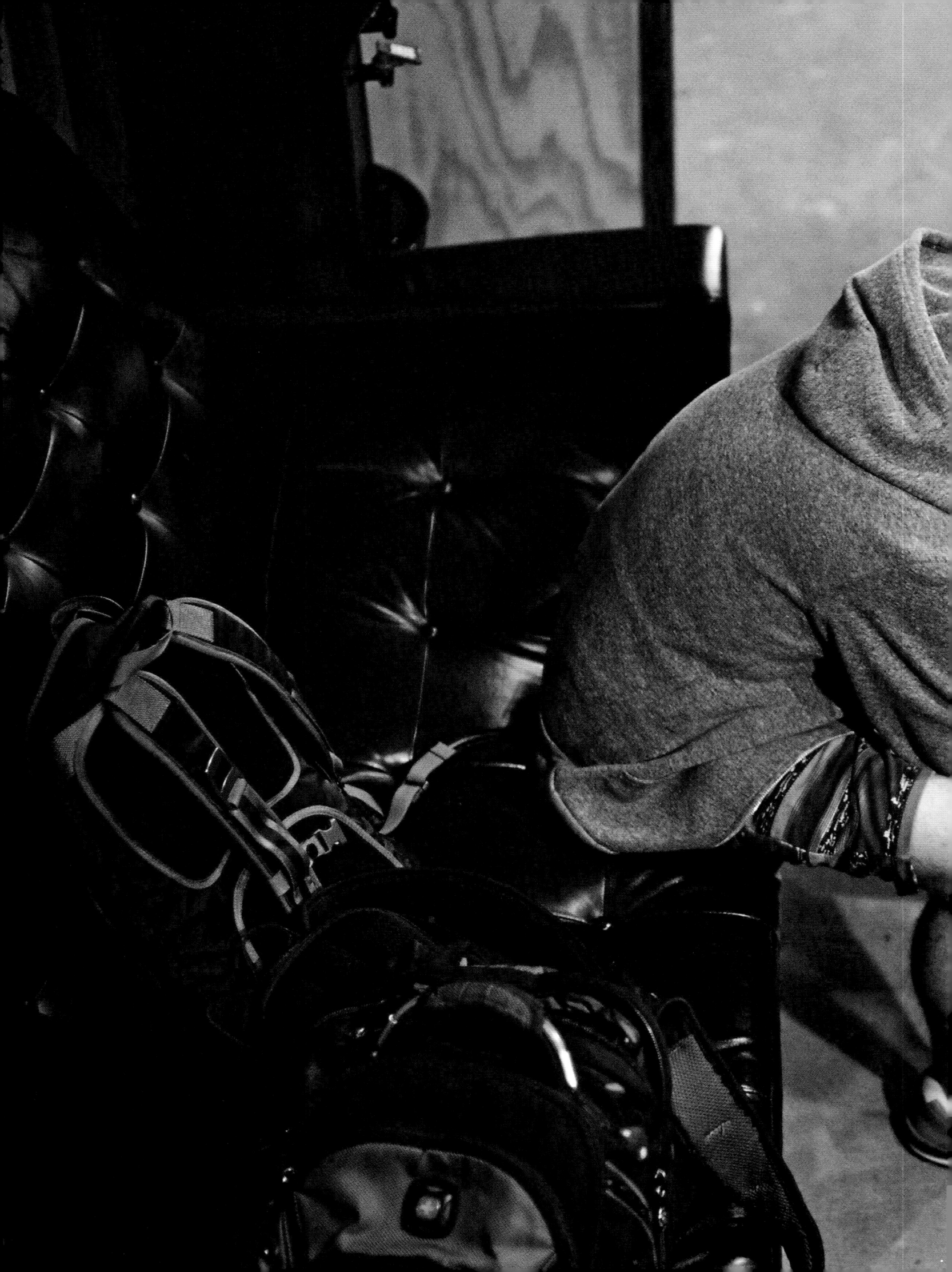

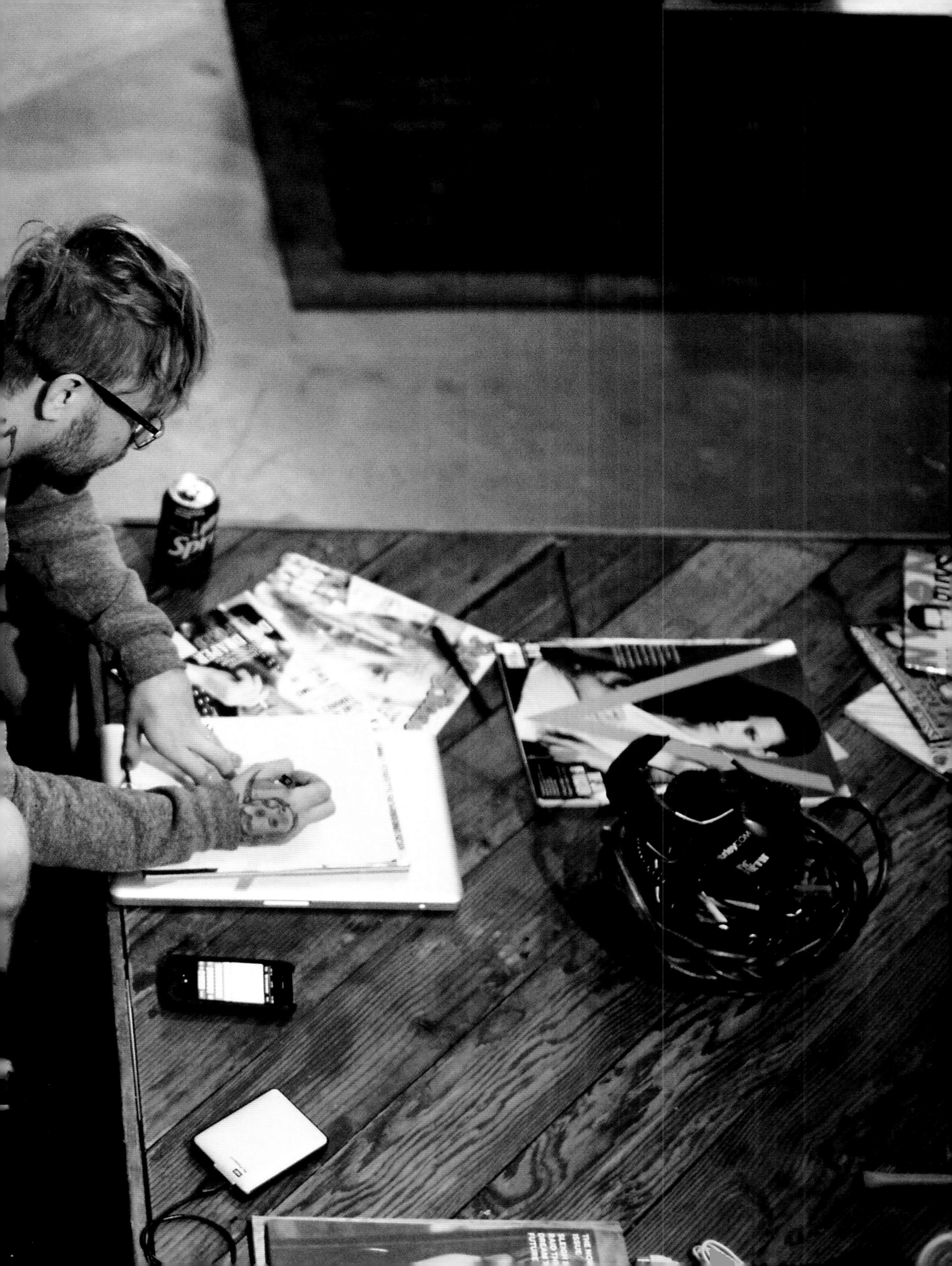

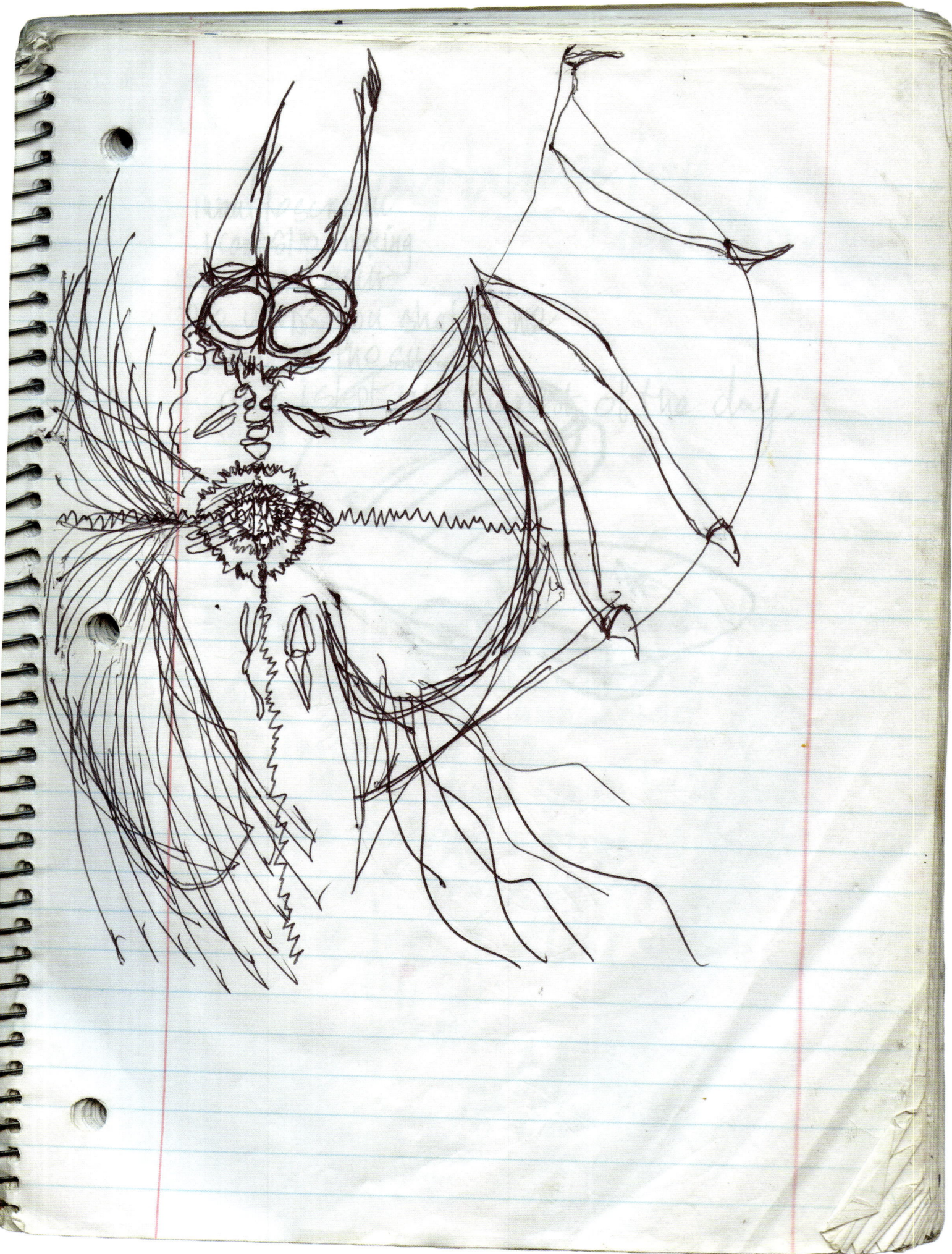

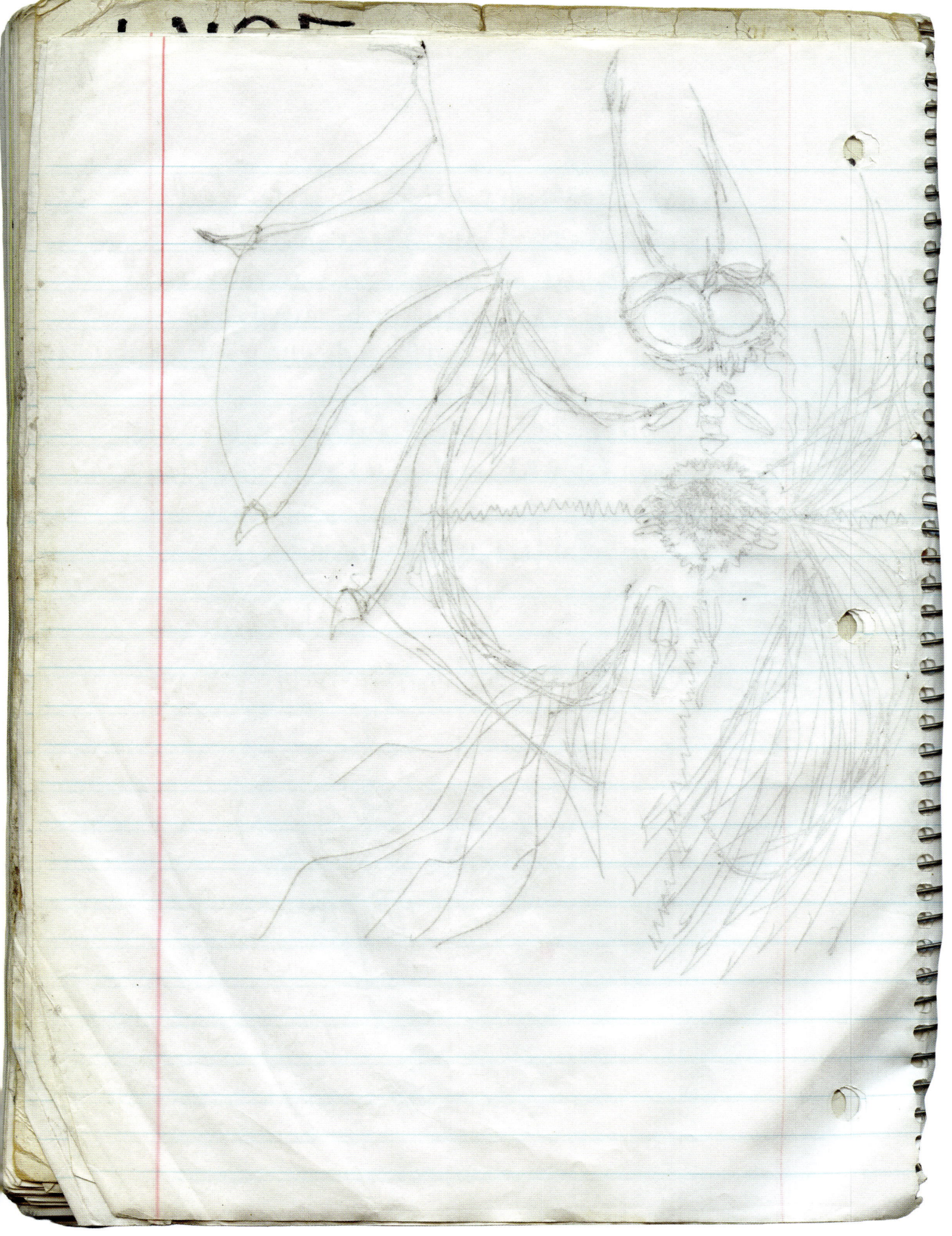

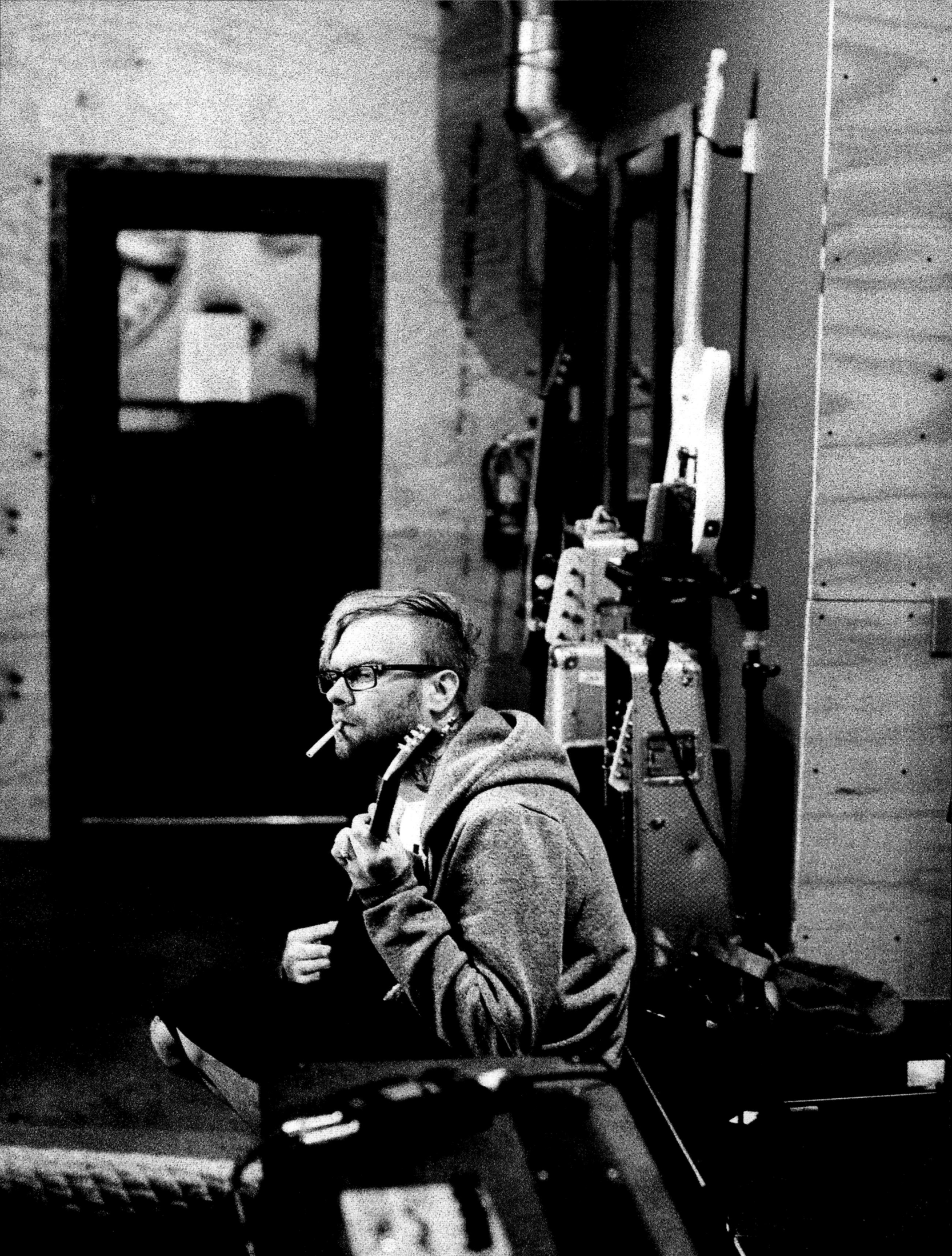

i want to scream
i can't stop shaking
something sour
the words you shot at me
shot down the sun
and i slept out the rest of the day.

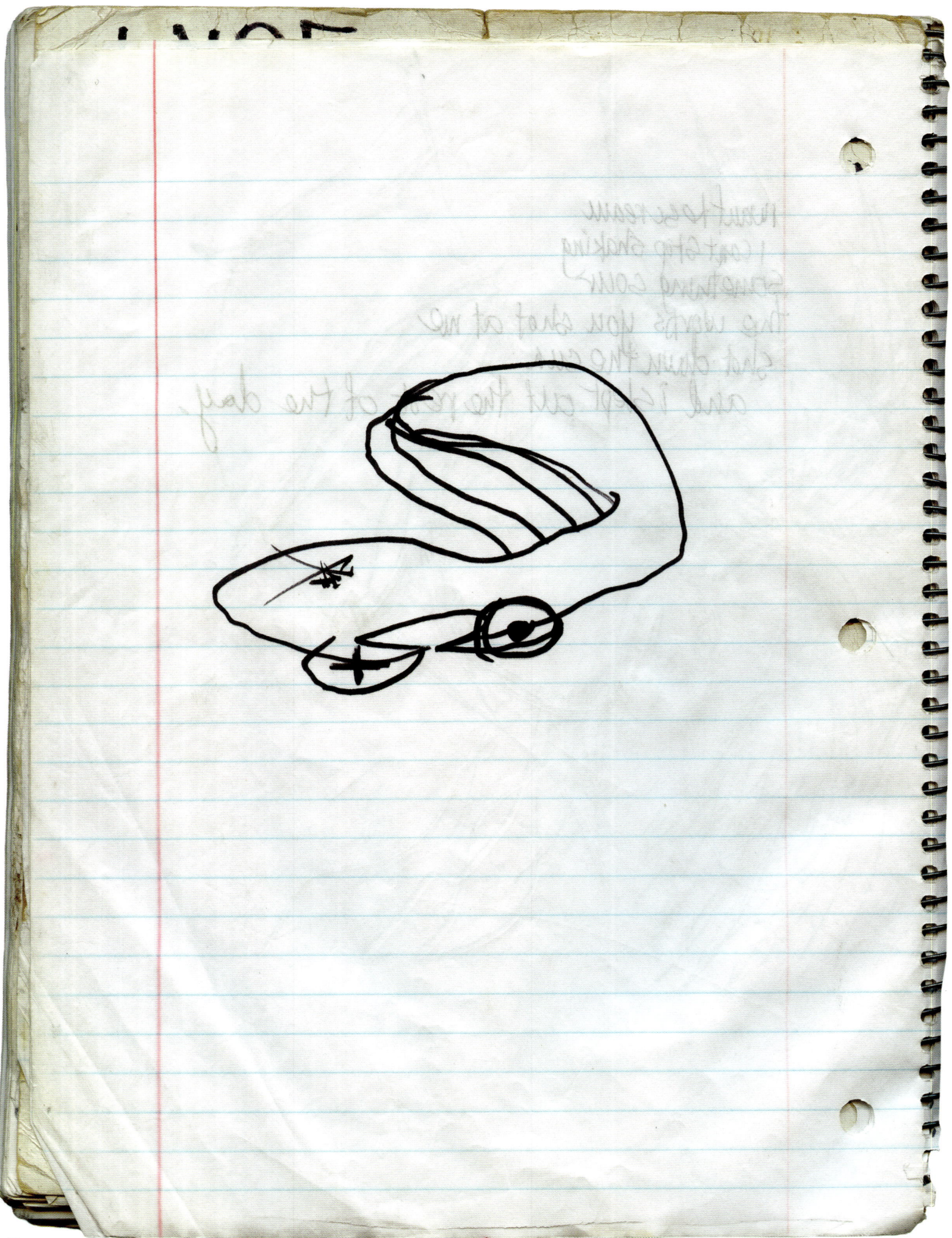

long before the
cigeretts.

first off F

i guess i remember every glance
you and shot me
thrkale. lastime unharmed
im loosing the
weight and some body heat
i say squse so hard i stopped your
heart from beating.
So deep that it didnt even
bleed.
catch me

We tracked down
the original friend
who had contact
with the...luckily I
had a friend outside
of the whole circle
who knew the kid
who was selling the
journal.

We met with him
and nicely asked
him to please give
me my journal back
and he agreed.

so deep that it didn't even bleed
caught me off guard red handed
now im far from lonely
(v1) asleep i still see you lying next
to me
so deep that it didnt even
bleed catch me.
oh. oh
i need anything else would
someone please just give me.
hit me knock me out and let
me go back to sleep
i can laugh all i want
inside i still am empty
so deep that i didnt even
scream.
fuck me fuck me. fuck me
(ch) i'll be just fine pretending im not
i'm far from lonely and its all
that i got
pretending.

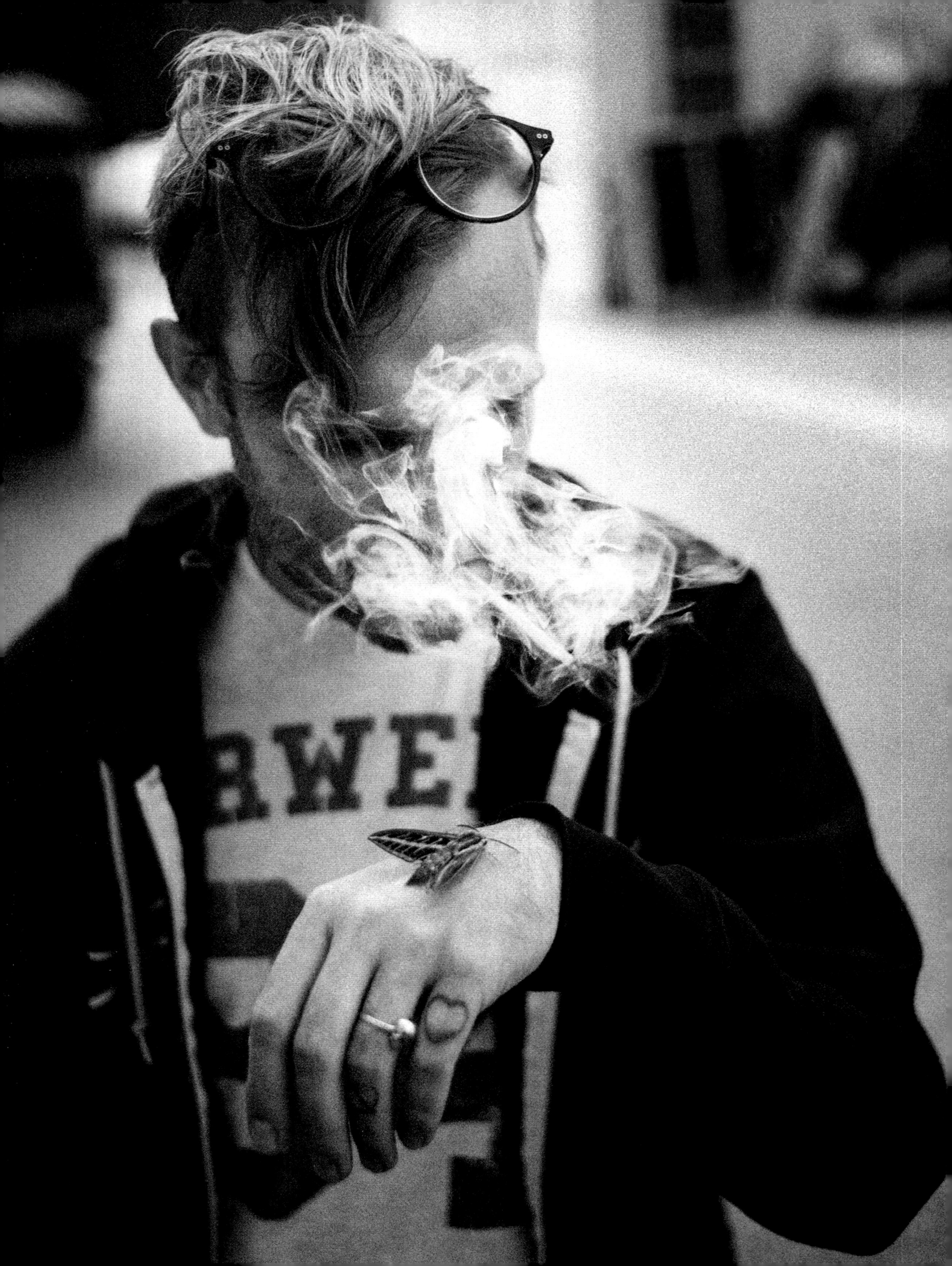

would you notice the way i held my toung
cutting fingers slip its hard to pay back all
the beggers like the oneuy you made
me baby take off your head
if you like it take a swing and a stab
get a cab follow breadcrumbs or
and end up all wet again.
early often ists the use of the thing
that turn on to abuse of your
face with the box my love.
im not speaking from experience
im a hyperite but at least
i dont petne anymore
scream.
and we can always hang just keep
throwing the small stones now
mama dont couse you know someday
one of us will leave with the nicest
parting gifts and the other ends
up in the hospital.
maybe if its not impossible to explode
than i'll just let my insides
go everwhere

send a long Rope
    Down this hole
to help me choke out
        all this
            dying.

theres nothing i can say
    you only hear what you want to
        maybe things are working quite a lot
better this way
        with the barrel of the gun
            pointed at you.

theres nothing i can say
    theres nothing i can do
its dead so bury it
    Just leave my heart
        alone.
    Just leave my heart
            alone

I found out through a friend that it was online for $10,000 and yeah, getting it back, I just had a friend, this kid was kind of struggled with addiction, so we met up with him at an AA meeting and he was kind enough to return the journal.

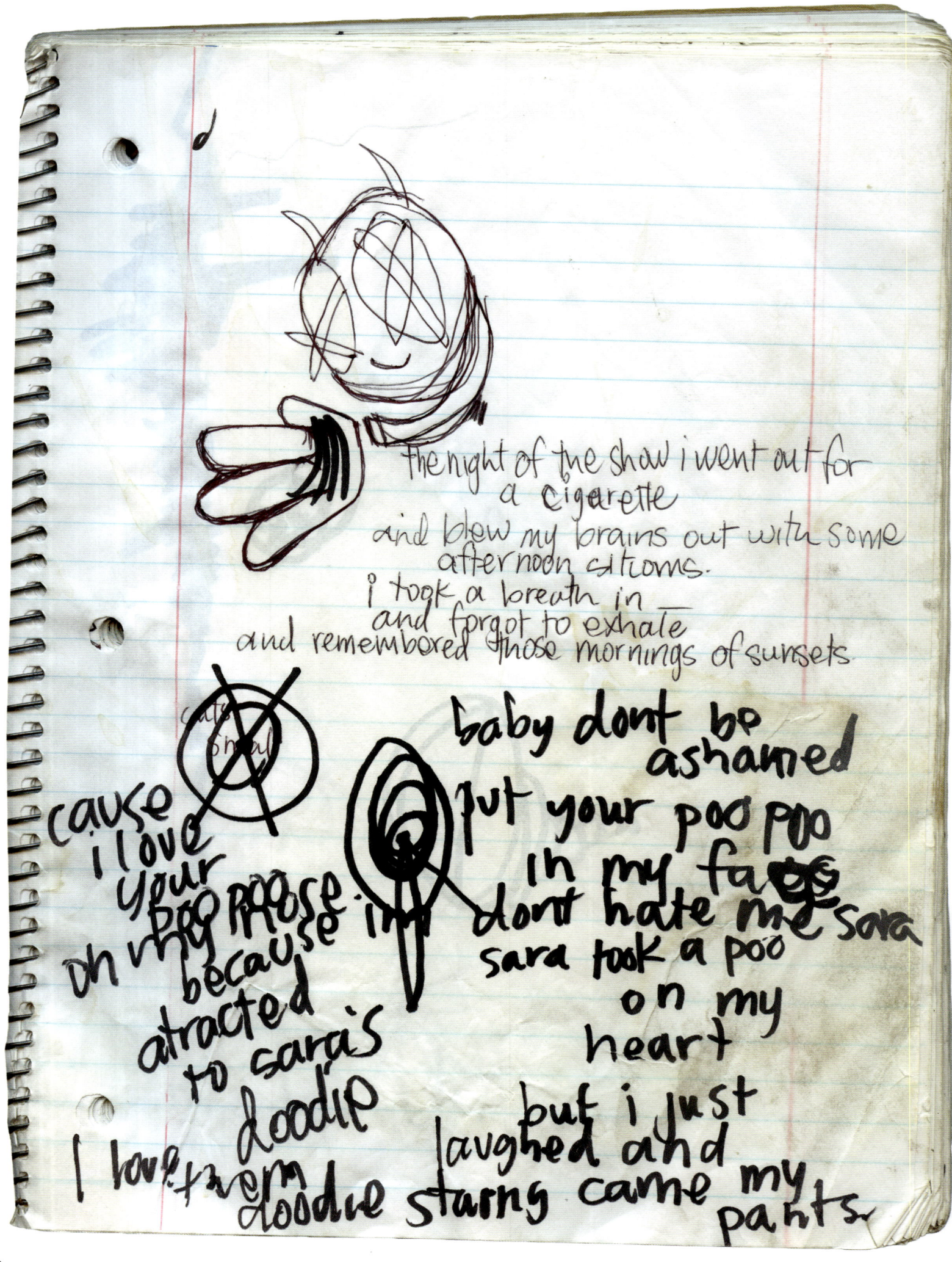

the night of the show i went out for a cigarette
and blew my brains out with some afternoon sitcoms.
i took a breath in
and forgot to exhale
and remembered those mornings of sunsets

baby dont be ashamed
put your poo poo in my face

cause i love your poo poo
oh why because im atracted to sara's doodie

i love them doodie

dont hate me sara
sara took a poo on my heart
but i just laughed and doodie starns came my pants.

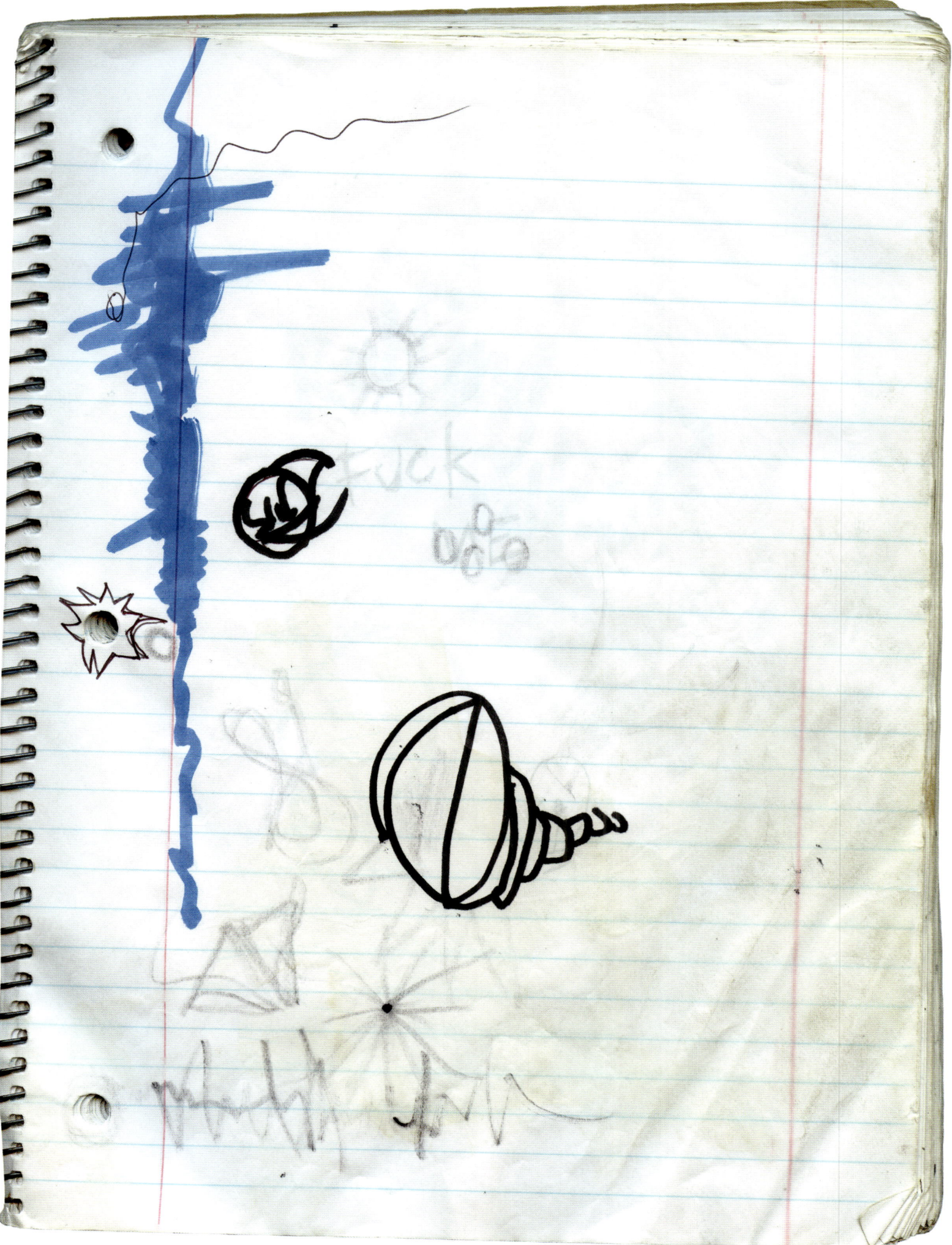

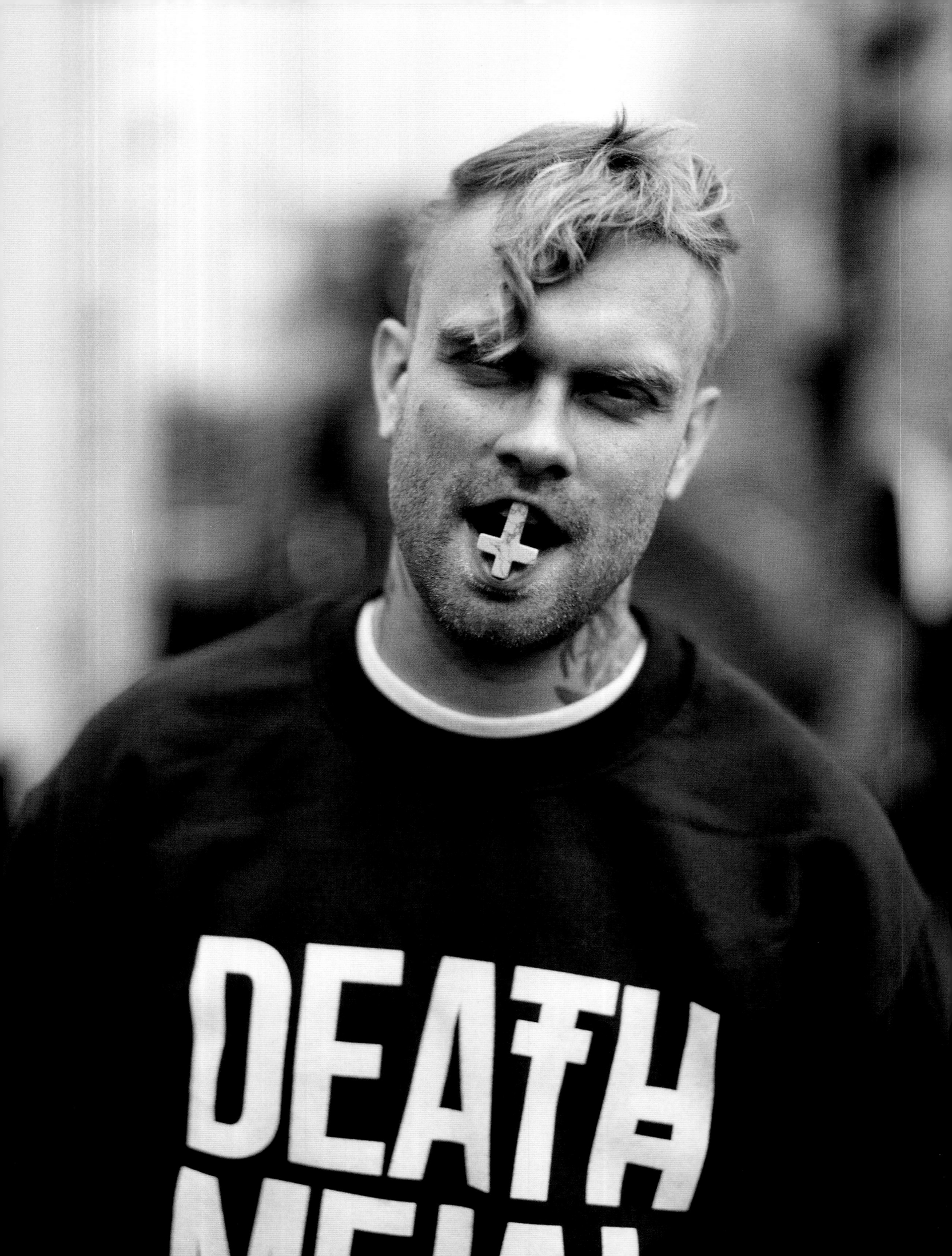

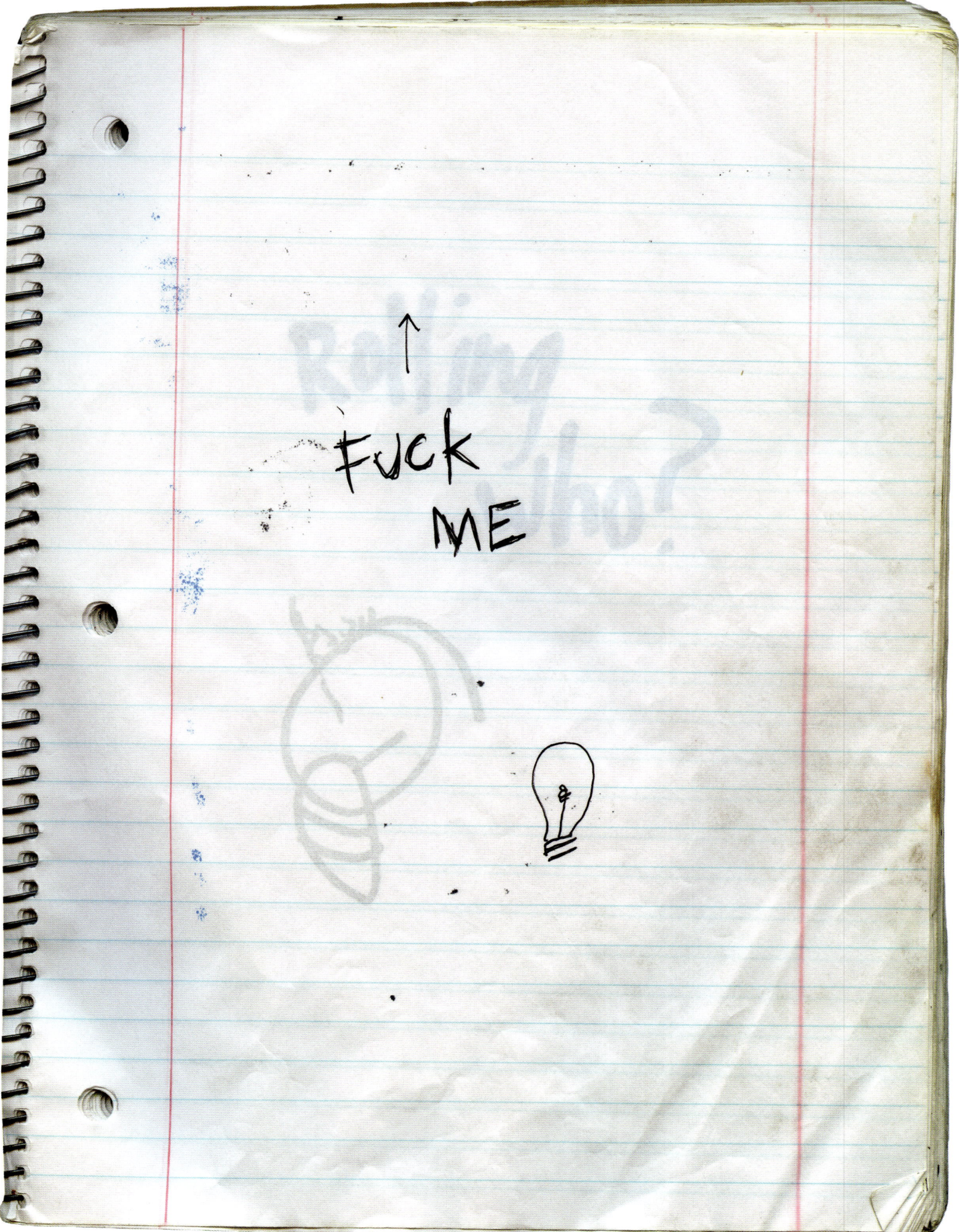

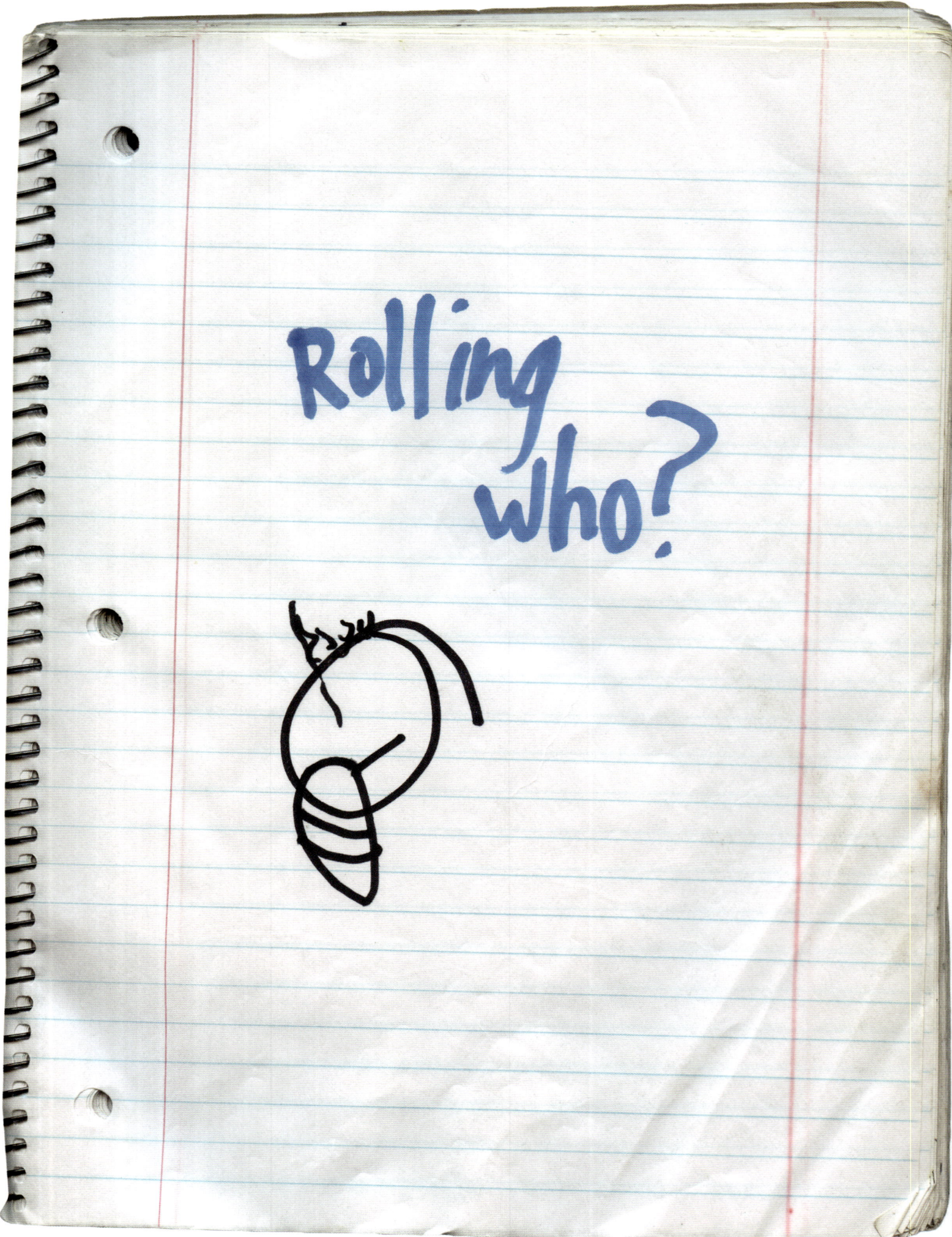

It'd been at least ten years. I remember looking around for the journal and thinking that it's probably just at the bottom of this box, and then when I searched further realizing it wasn't there, freaked out, but it had been another at least five or six years since we saw it surface online.

more generic screamo songs
i guess i know huh
whatever.

(but not really)

when will all of it happen to them
in their screams echo sounds of
the living

the fire department couldnt drown the city
but jesus made it a point to stop me
my web streaches

as far as i can tell
im picking up the pieces
im walking out the door
do i care to make a point
as love engages war.
a beautiful machinist
a perfect type
of war.

In the beginning of the recording processes for maybe the first four or five records, it was always about a journal and always keeping it compact and all in the same place and tight so I could search around and find what I'm looking for easily or pull from poems that aren't necessarily part of political content yet. The journal was very, very important to me. It's like a time capsule that lets me travel back in time to 2004 and be a part of the young me who was crazy unruly.

(ch) in the quiet it happened
         and it wasnt so pretty
      cut my eyballs out of my head
cause idont need to see
      In the quiet it happened
      and id wasnt so pretty
i can see see see more
   clearly now
there is no love in SAnity

learn to READ
speak in tongues

v1· learn to read
 speak in toungs
make no habit as a rule of thumb
 express your anger in small and selfish ways.
fear almost informally
 keep an eyeball on you ~~olo~~ sanity
 ~~camel~~ and measure up you calories
 and try spending casually

 v2 dont fuck dont fight
youvegoto sleep at night
 stay organized and try keep it tight
 ~~only speak~~ hoy hoy hey

 the rules
 the schools
 the lines behind
 the guys with ties
that ~~and~~ recognize that
 life is work
 success is not a state
 of
 mind

 ha ha ha

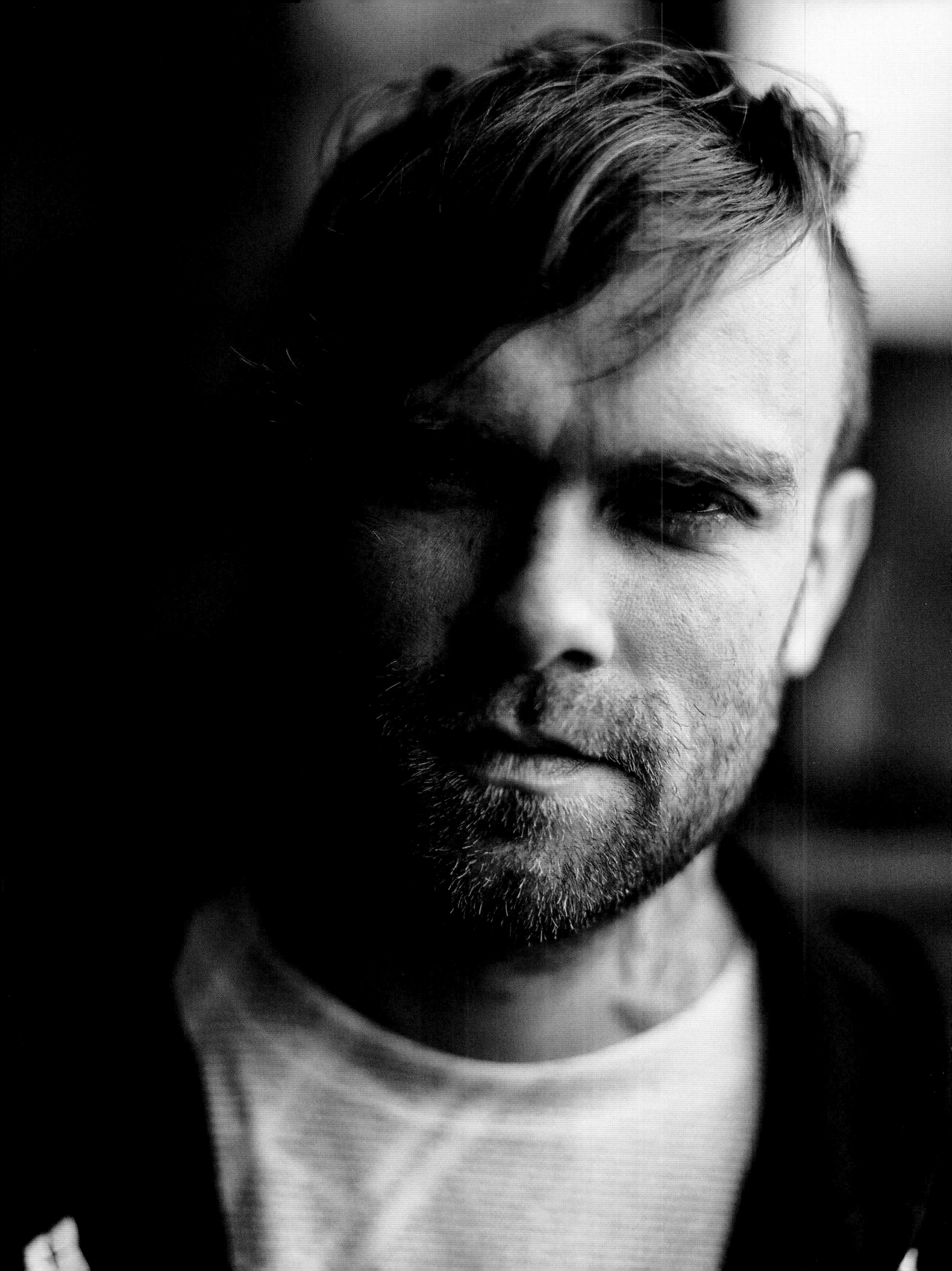

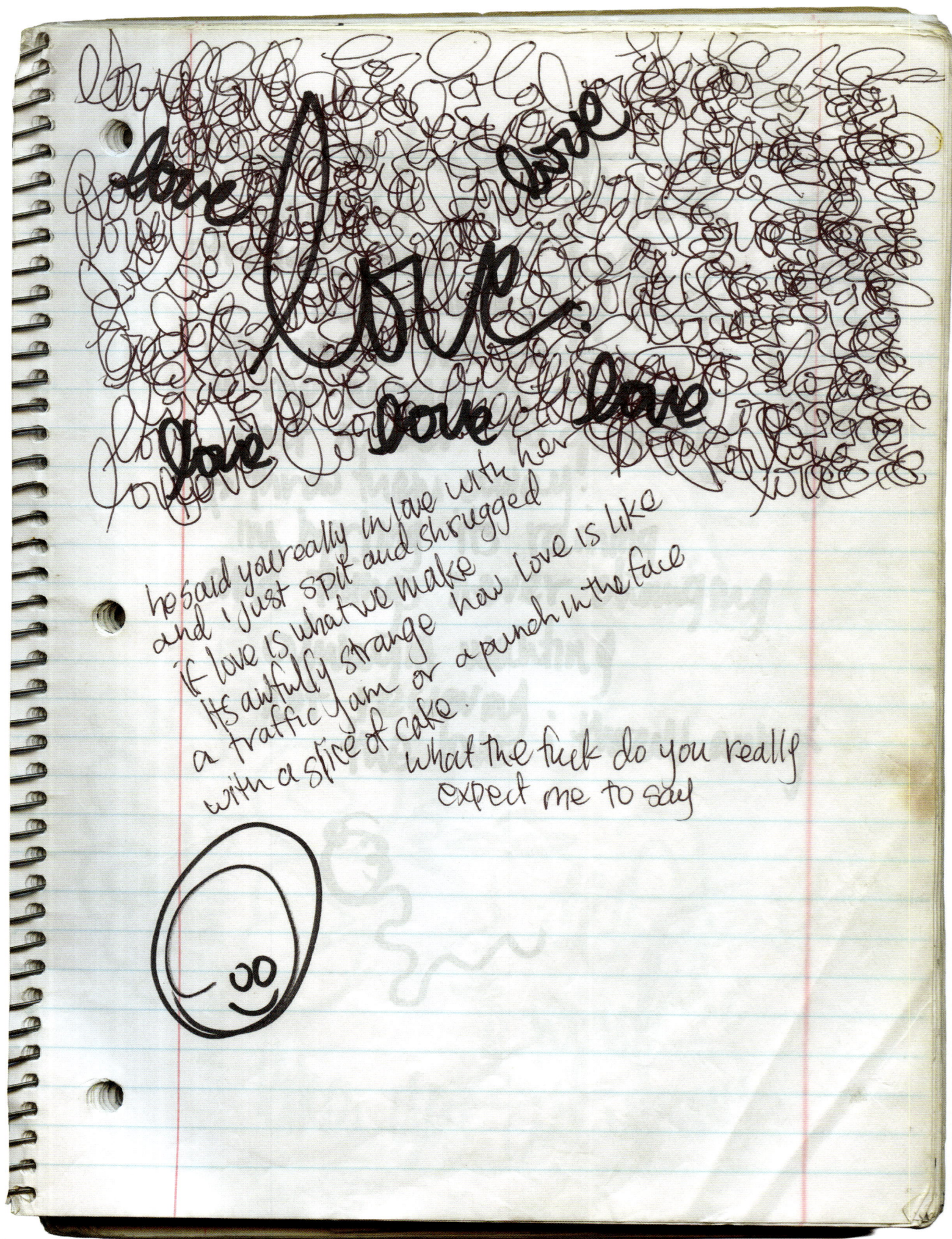

he said you really in love with her
and i just spit and shrugged
if love is what we make
its awfully strange how love is like
a traffic jam or a punch in the face
with a slice of cake.

what the fuck do you really
expect me to say

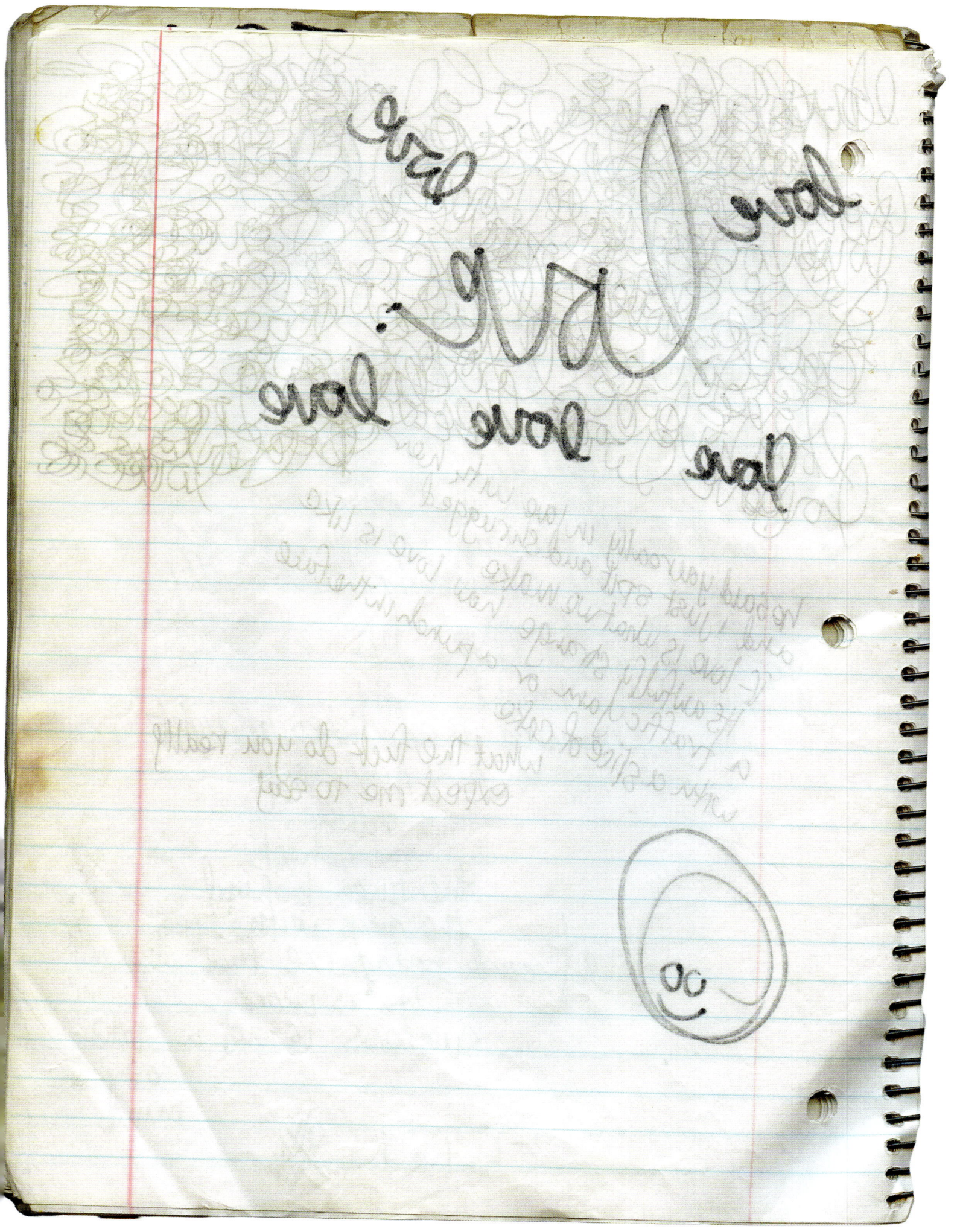

I feel stuck ~~staring~~
    Straight out of luck
straight out of love
    an unwanted fuck
you make me sick
    the memories fade
    but never to quickly
to throw them away.
    im hurting its raining
and things never changing
    always wanting
not recieving
        the love i threw away

I feel like the whole process of writing down lyrics has kind of disappeared in the last ten years. I think that everybody does it digitally. It's easier to share notes that way and whatever, but I still try to keep written journals. I find it's more personal when I'm writing it down, actually pen writing and yeah, it's a great way to keep it all together and keep it in one place.

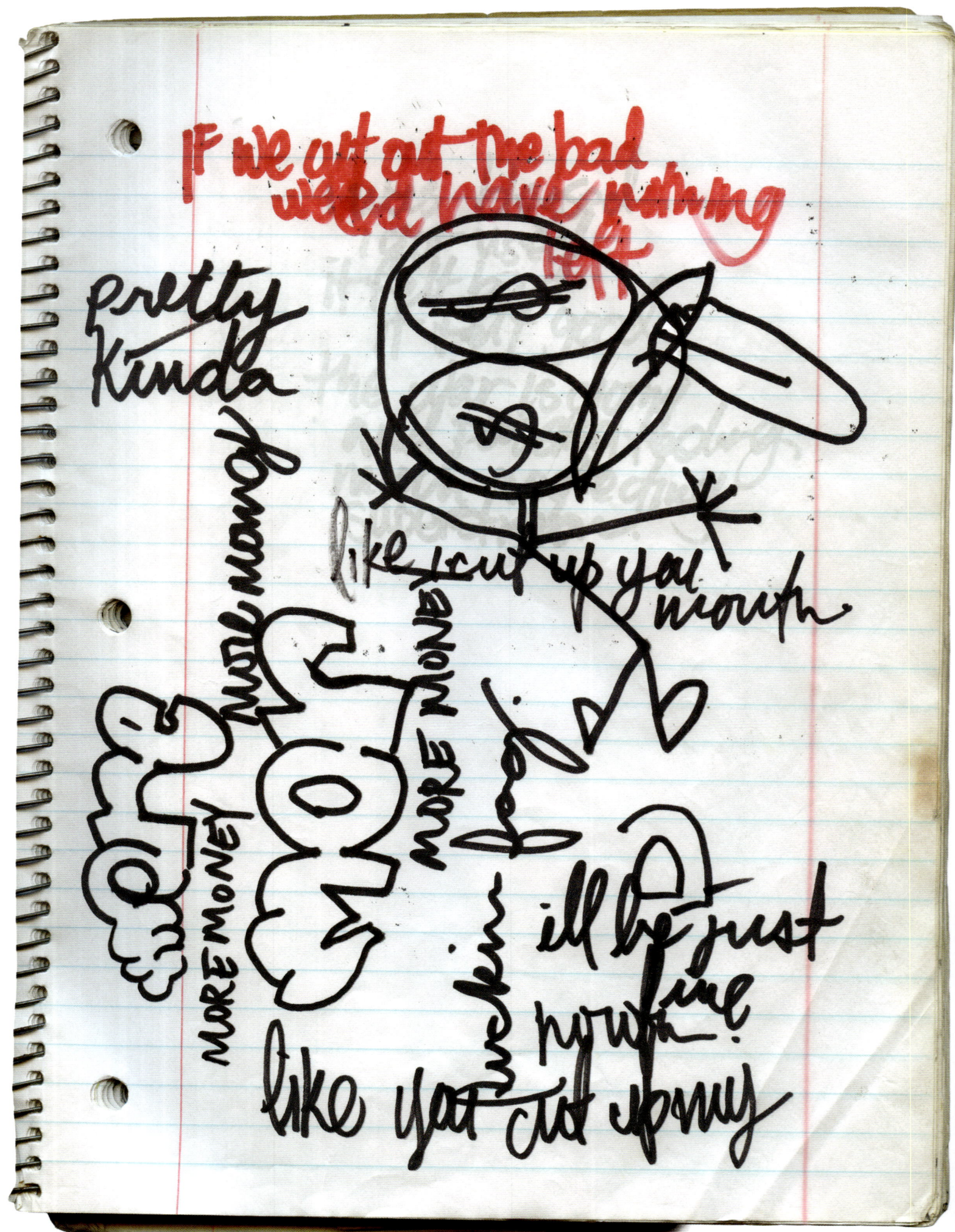

i was blessed
i got used
it felt bad
it felt good
the war is going
and passing, fading
much neglecting
superstition.

with the prints that they took at the station
  I swollowed an eraser
119 dollar express
this place is quite clean
but I guess it was just me
  for one night and of corse I decided
to stay all the same
if I felt different. about all of it
I did it for her face...

watched you bite into
the bottle
~~watched~~ watched me kick
out the chair.
I let you chew up the glass
and laughed
as you just hung there.
I had thought of rose pedals
mostly perfectly pure
And then I thought of
your ~~flower~~ pedals
and all the abuse
they've been
through

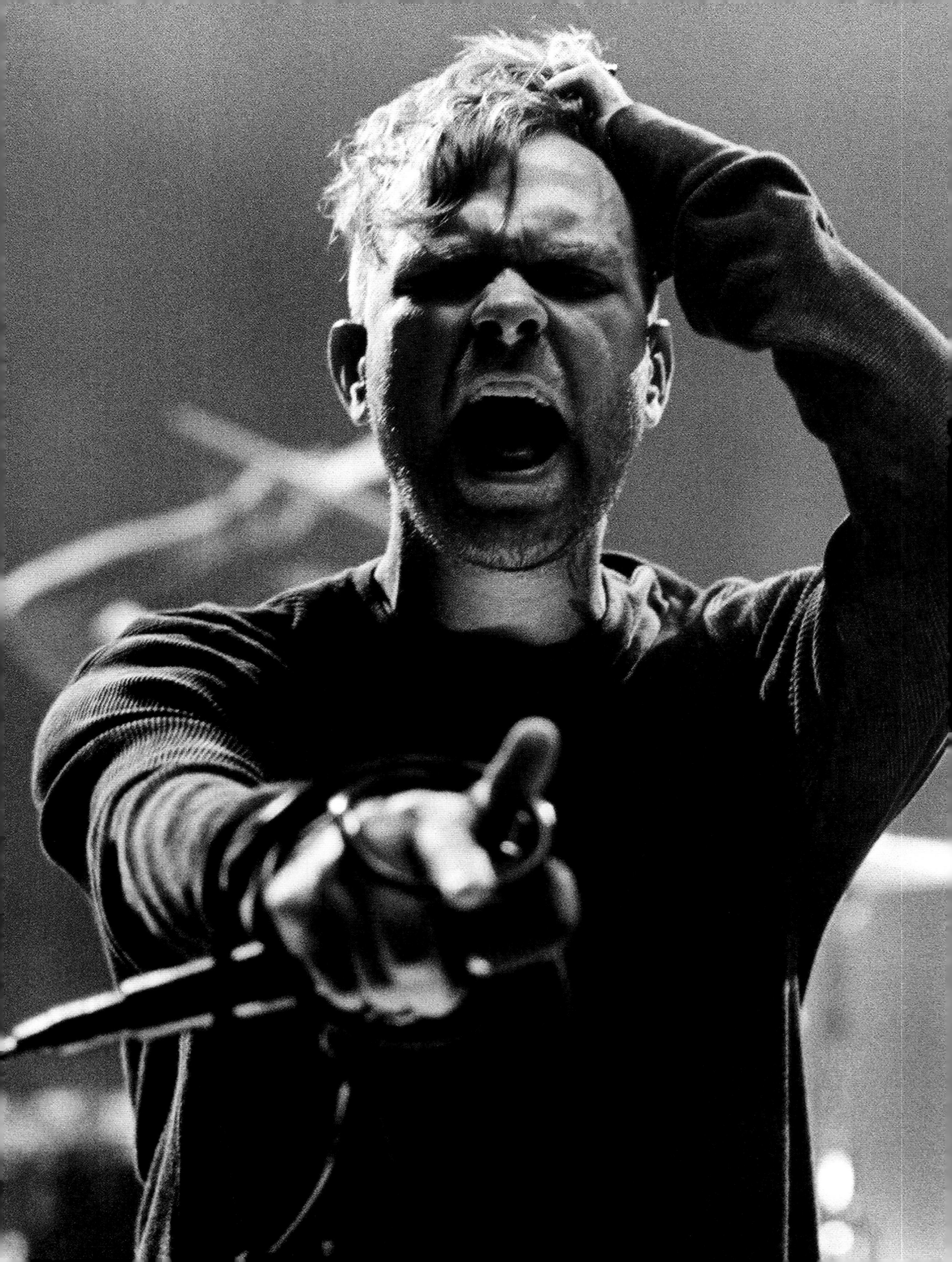

the way you shot your eyes at me
your unexpect sandry
the way you shot your eyes at
me
your gone but all around you are
my eyes are red im saving face
the way you shot your eyes at
me

you a pretty good shot

besides its fun fun
and ● we all have a job to do

i understand how i felt
how i feel, how i am feeling
putting you through this
fucking you like this

one way i learned
never to return
I know I will shedd last

its an embarrasing
in some cases   terrible   horrible
its better to leave   knight
the room.   more

no matter how much we
         try
and matter how much we
            play
it alway comes out always
                sounding so pretty

and a 1 2 3 and 1 2 1 2 3
will I be the last one shedding
         look at me   I get to stay

lets just have fun ok
its hedious
absently hedious
of what its
happening

im sure its for the
best i mean im
so sorry.

I cant believe its happening
I was last

It's all over the place for me. A lot of personal stuff, a lot of thoughts and reflections. I read a lot. So a lot of books that I'm reading are kind of parts that I love or moments that I would take away. So probably a lot of personal stuff in there. Thoughts and random scattered ideas.

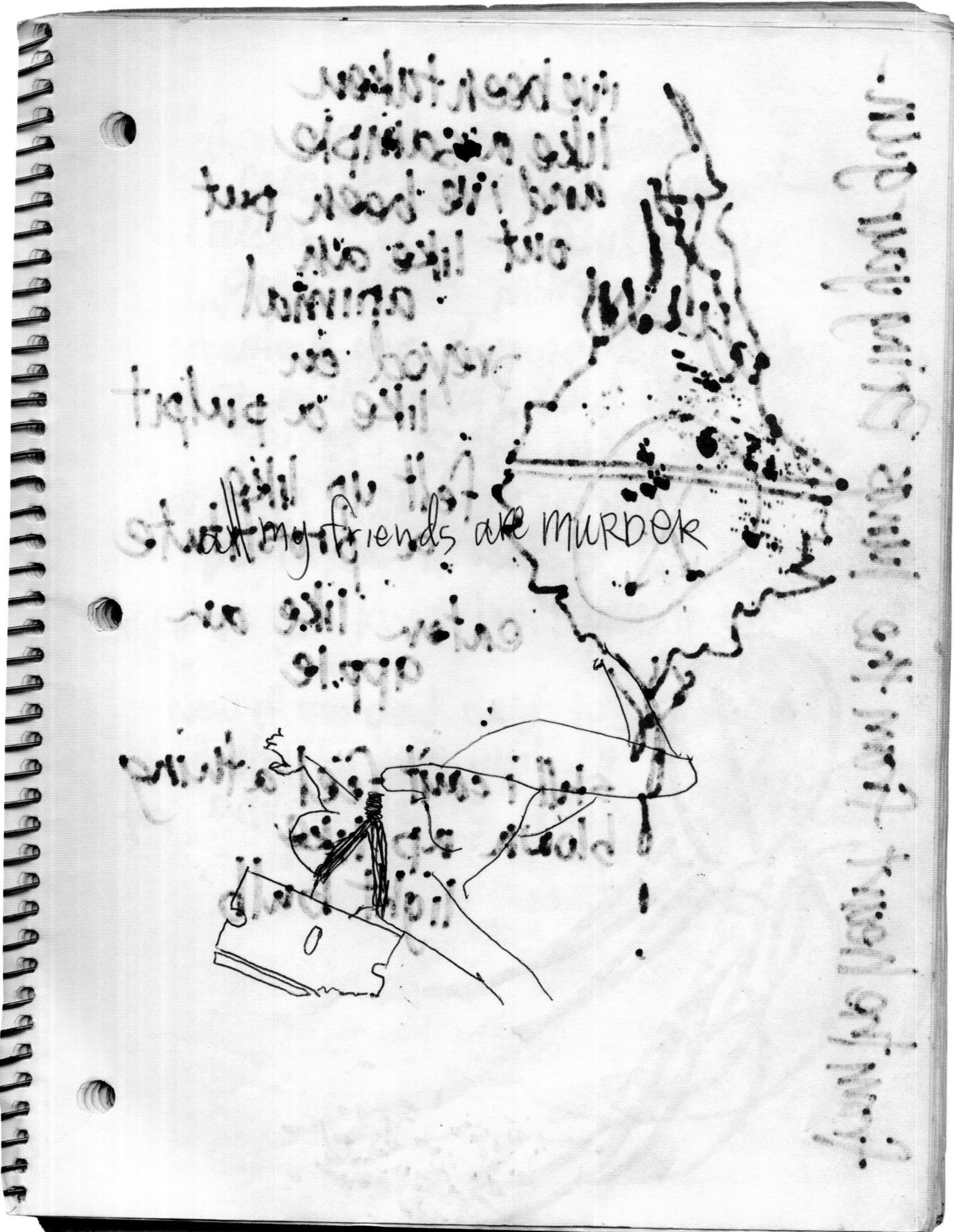

all my friends are MURDER

i've been taken
like a sample
and i've been put
out like an
        animal
preyed on
    like a pulpit
felt up like
    a prostitute
eaten like an
    apple

still i can't feel a thing
blown up like
    light bulb

from the heart — from the lungs Bring your gun —

when i called you my angel
i meant more like a ghost
cause you leave and leave
and leave invisible.
feeling you change the insides
of my body, and your
secrets safe with me
cause you know that im willing to
be taken it makes me
cause you know I will give it up
honestly.
now if you dont want to love me
i'll still be here waiting
for. advantage is givin and taken

I think it was the first time I tried to read *Infinite Jest* in 2004 and I made it maybe halfway through. I didn't finish the book until 2010 or 2011. I always tried to read the most convoluted and complicated books, including *Gravity's Rainbow*.

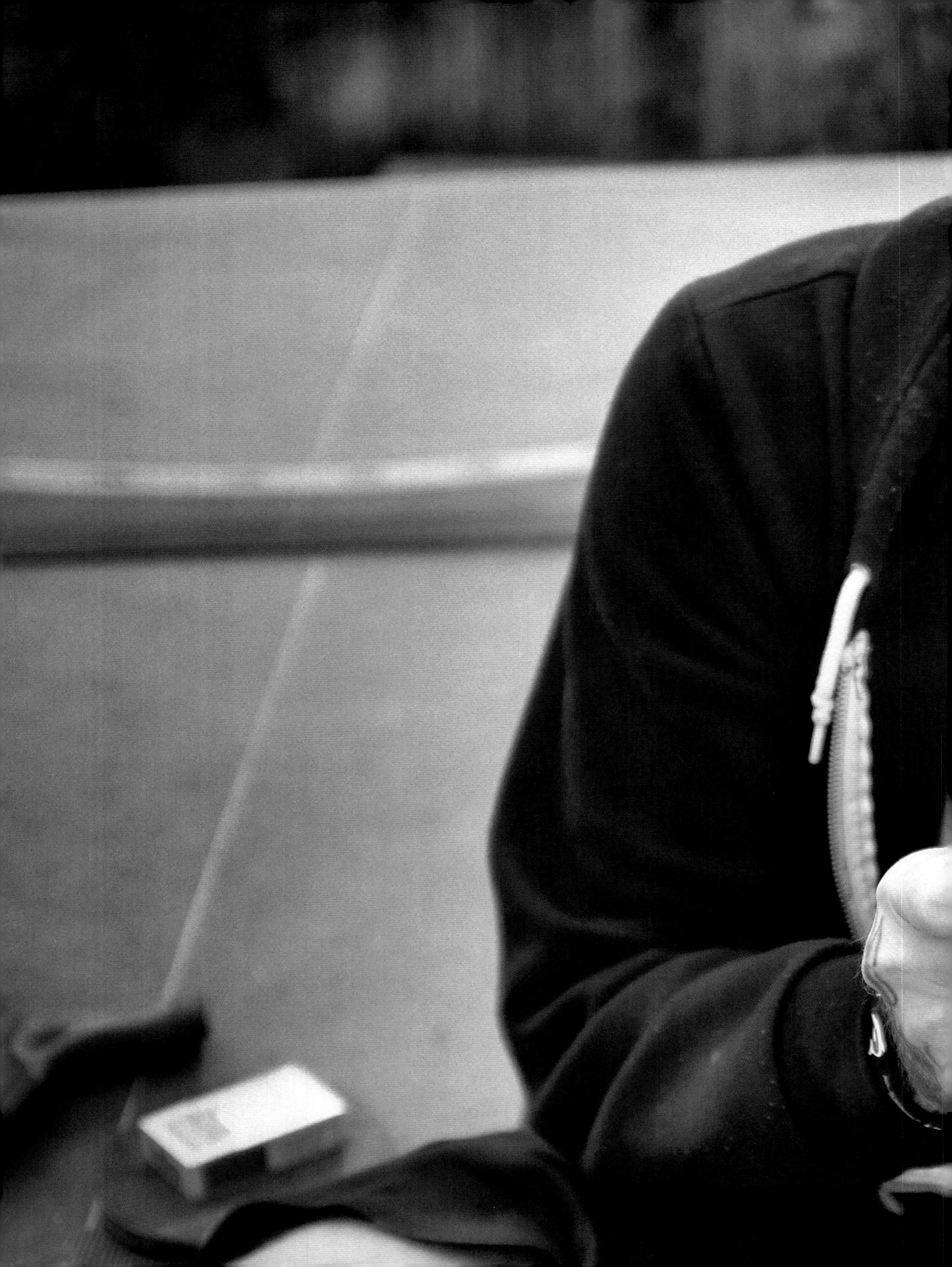

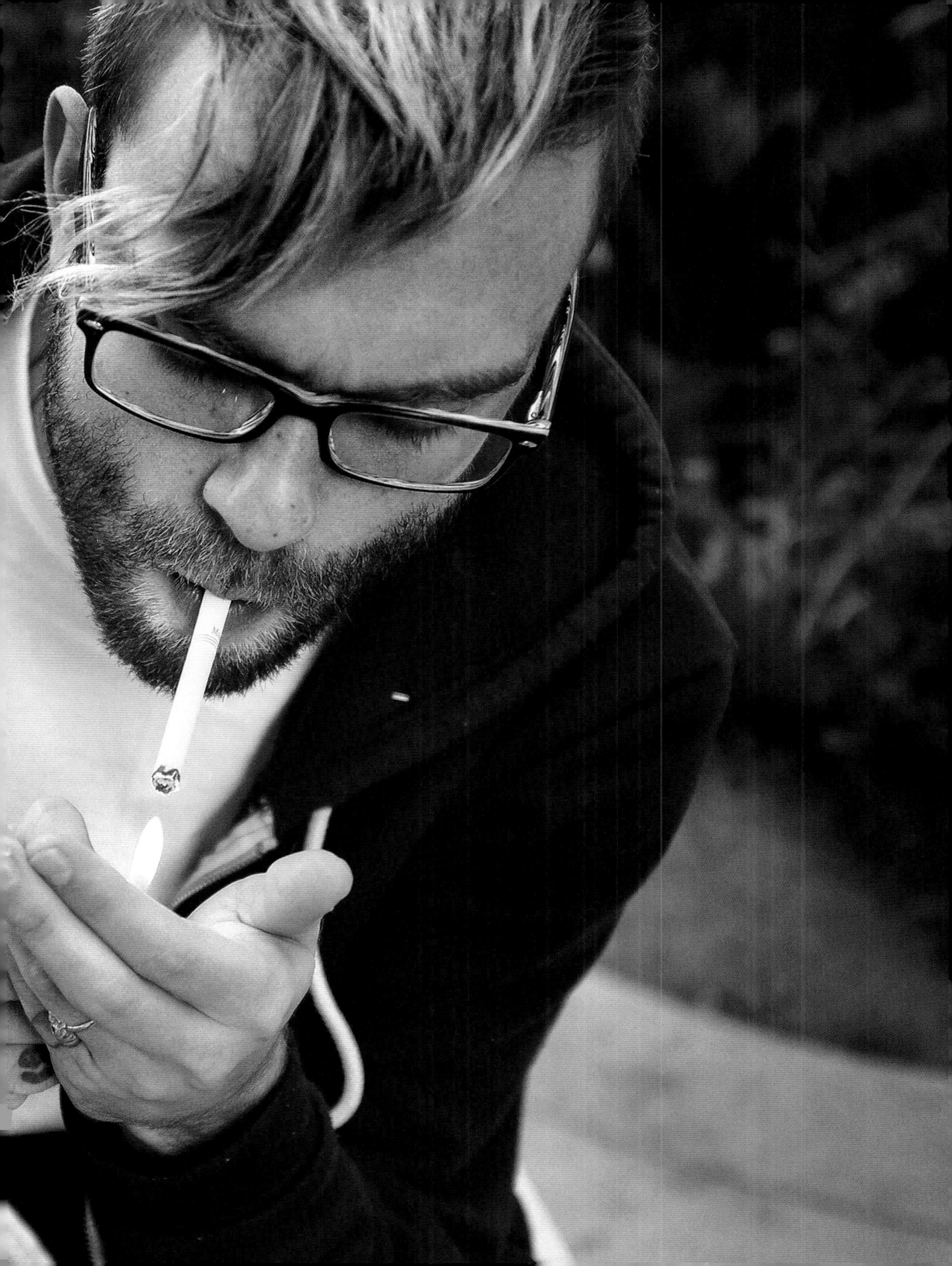

when I called you my angel
I meant more like a ghost
cause you leave and leave
and leave invisible.
feeling you change the insides
of my body and your
sweat soak with me
cause you know that im willing to
be taken it makes me
cause you know I will give it up
honestly.
now if you dont want to love me
i'll still be here waiting
for. advantage is givin and takin

you skins attach
this fragile cliche
of a crooked
smiling back
you could

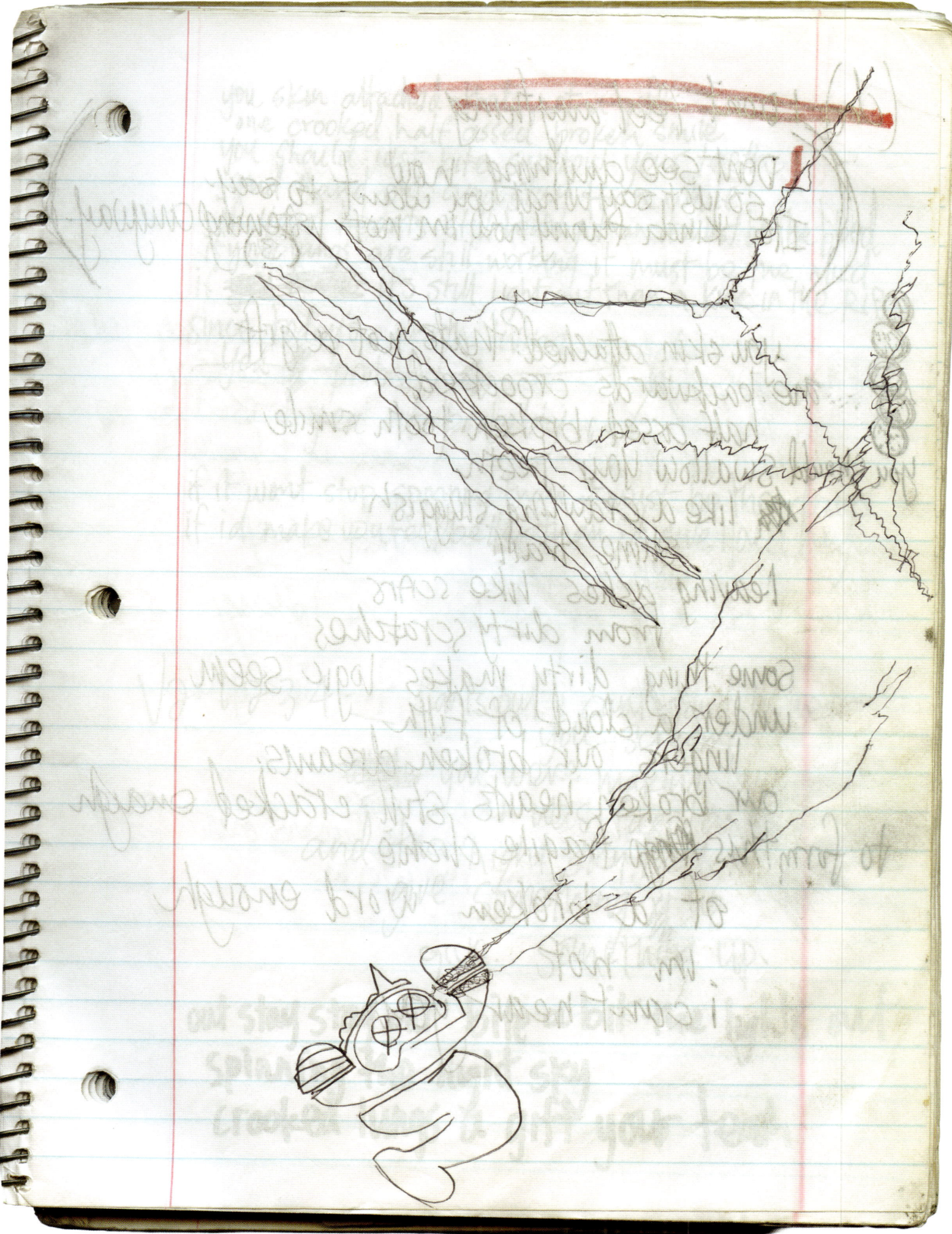

(ch) I Dont feel anything
I Dont see anything now
so just say what you want to say.
Its kinda funny how im not listening anyway. (3)

you skin attached? thats not a gift
are backwards croocked
half assed broken tooth smile
you should swallow your teeth
like a crawling sluggish
slime trail
leaving ashes like scars
from dirty scratches
some thing dirty makes logic seem
under a cloud of filth
lingers our broken dreams.
our broken hearts still cracked enough
to form this fragile cliché
of a broken word enough
. im not
i cant hear you.

you skin attached thats not a gift
one crooked half assed broken smile
you should just bite swallow your teeth
and hang out and stay for a while.
if your hearts still beating than it must be the blood
if your lungs are still working it must be the mud
if ~~you~~ its still light out than a kick in the RIBS
since todays worth living
~~yea probably~~ →
              yea if probably is

if it wont stop spinning than it must be the drugs
if id make you feel better than id give you a hug.

V2 1 2 3 4 ~~two~~ lights out i cant stand to hear
                        you scream
        ~~while~~ you were making love
                i was fast asleep
        and the night sky better
        give something up

              give. something up.

out stay stay out bite a bit the lights out
spinning the night sky
crooked lungs a gift your teeth

There are the first pass of lyrics for "Let It Bleed." I remember sitting on John Feldman's floor in his studio and using his CD player to continue to rewind to write the lyrics out, which is really cool. You never use a CD player anymore. It was all CDs back then. We would take the recording for what we had, burn it down to a disc, and then I would sit in front of a CD player for hours and just try to work it out.

when i said scream you said
how come i turned my frown
you blew your brains out and
slit your wrists and wouldn't
leave
the singer finished singing and she walking out
the singer sheds a tear fear of falling out
my worries way the world has i used to be
and everything im cold seems a plague in
me

and its hard to say how i feel today
for years gone by
and i cried but not today

worse than a fear its the lie you

when i said scream you said how come
when you said leave i blew my brains out
early bird has caught the worm

out stay stay out bite a bit the lights out
spinning the night sky
crooked limbs a gift your teeth

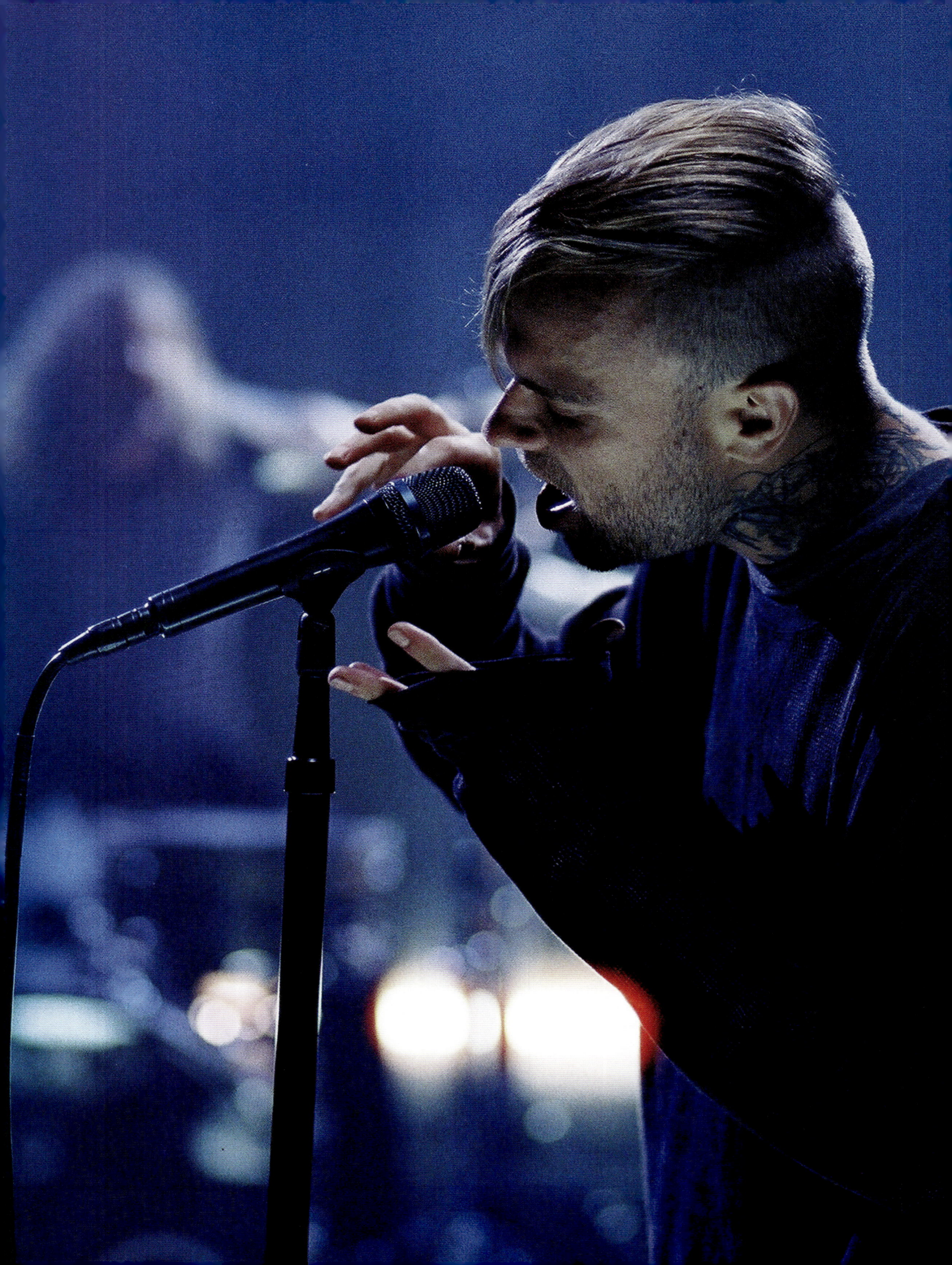

i just want to touch your face
eat those words that i've wasted
and taste you
although some of my strikes wont erase
I know all my dreams worth the chase

fuck
i fuck fuck
fuck
fuck
FUCK
fuck
Barb

your in eyes in the shape
of my heart

(page number)

69

look at me
  you can tell
by the way i move and do my hair
  you can tell
  that its me
  or its not me i dont even care
i dont ~~even~~ im allright
  i dont smell
  im the cleanest i have ever been now.
i feel big
  i feel tall
      i feel dry
just look at me now
        im a fake
do i drink
  do i date
ive got perfect placement, all my ink
satisfied in your eyes
im the biggest fan ive got right now
i feel big   im ade sure that i look how i wanted to look
i feel tall   and the people around me
      the people surround me
my accesories. will keep me warm.

My stomack hurts now
  and so does my face
and its all im like all.

my stomake hurts now.
. and tied off in lace
i pray beg for anything
to hit me in the face
this sickness isnt me
i pray to fall from grace
~~crawl~~

the last thing i see is
feeling

when i ~~bright~~ stopped to call you my
little girl   i meant more
            so much more
~~these words im used to~~
than these words im so used to i used
them to use you. they want to
                    they want to
see the jaws drop as you fly like
a butterfly straight into my web.

The second pass of lyrics for "All That I've Got."
At the time I had a teacup chihuahua named
David Bowie, and when I flew out to record
the record, I booked the wrong airline. It's on
Southwest and they don't allow you to fly with
dogs. So I had my family watch the dog for two
days until he was going to be able to fly out that
weekend, and in the meantime he was hit by a car
and it totally wrecked my life. My little buddy, he
pretty much lived in my pocket, you know what I
mean? So yeah, wrecked my life and I didn't know
what to do about it except for write a song.
So "All That I've Got" is a song that kind of
encapsulates that whole moment in my life.

There are also the first couple passes for the lyrics
for "Cut Up Angels." I remember sitting in my car
quite a bit. The car was the usual place where I
would scam the CD over and over and over and
over and cut up Angels. This song is a rare one for
the use this song's about sex, which we never really
write about.

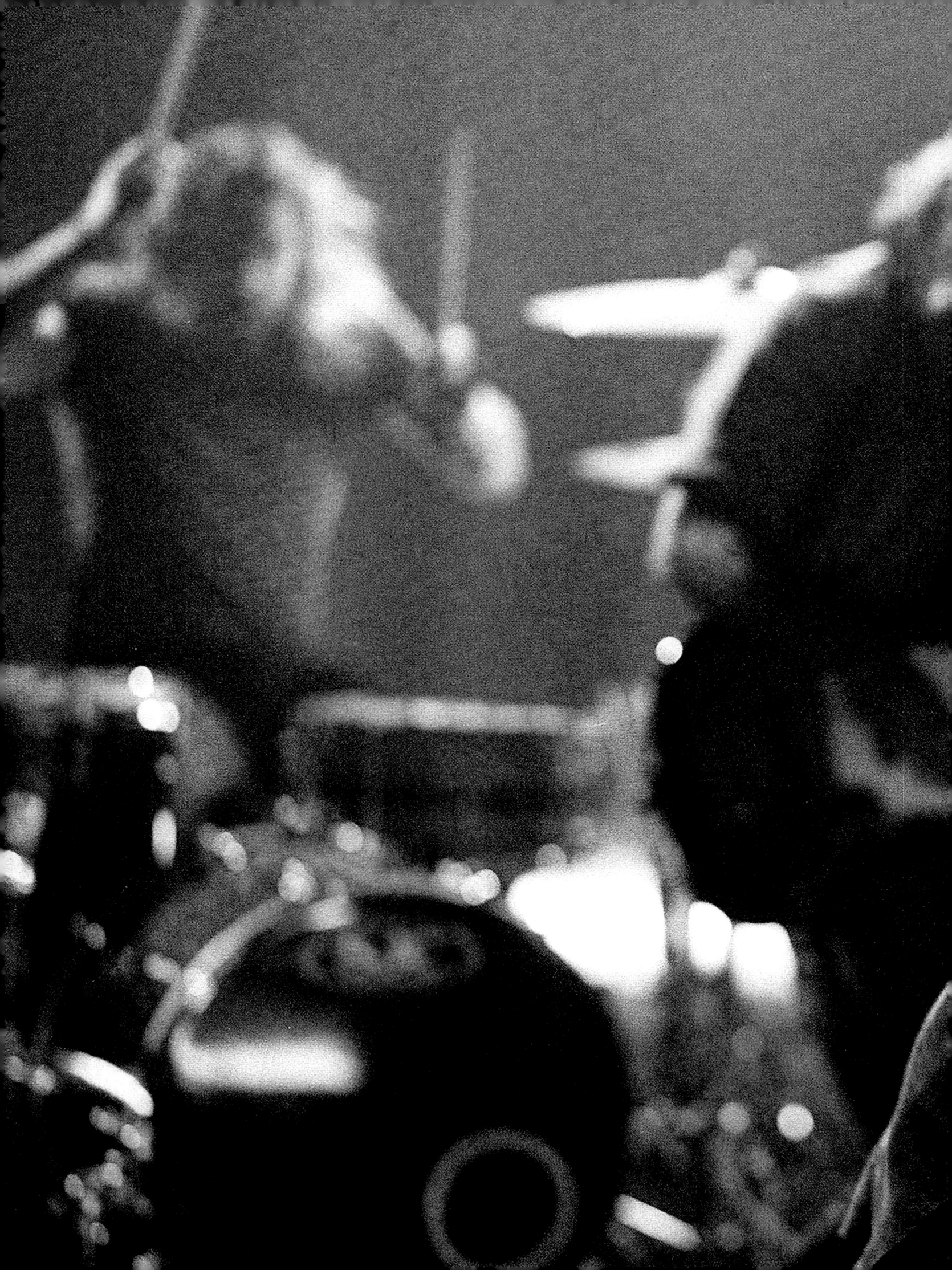

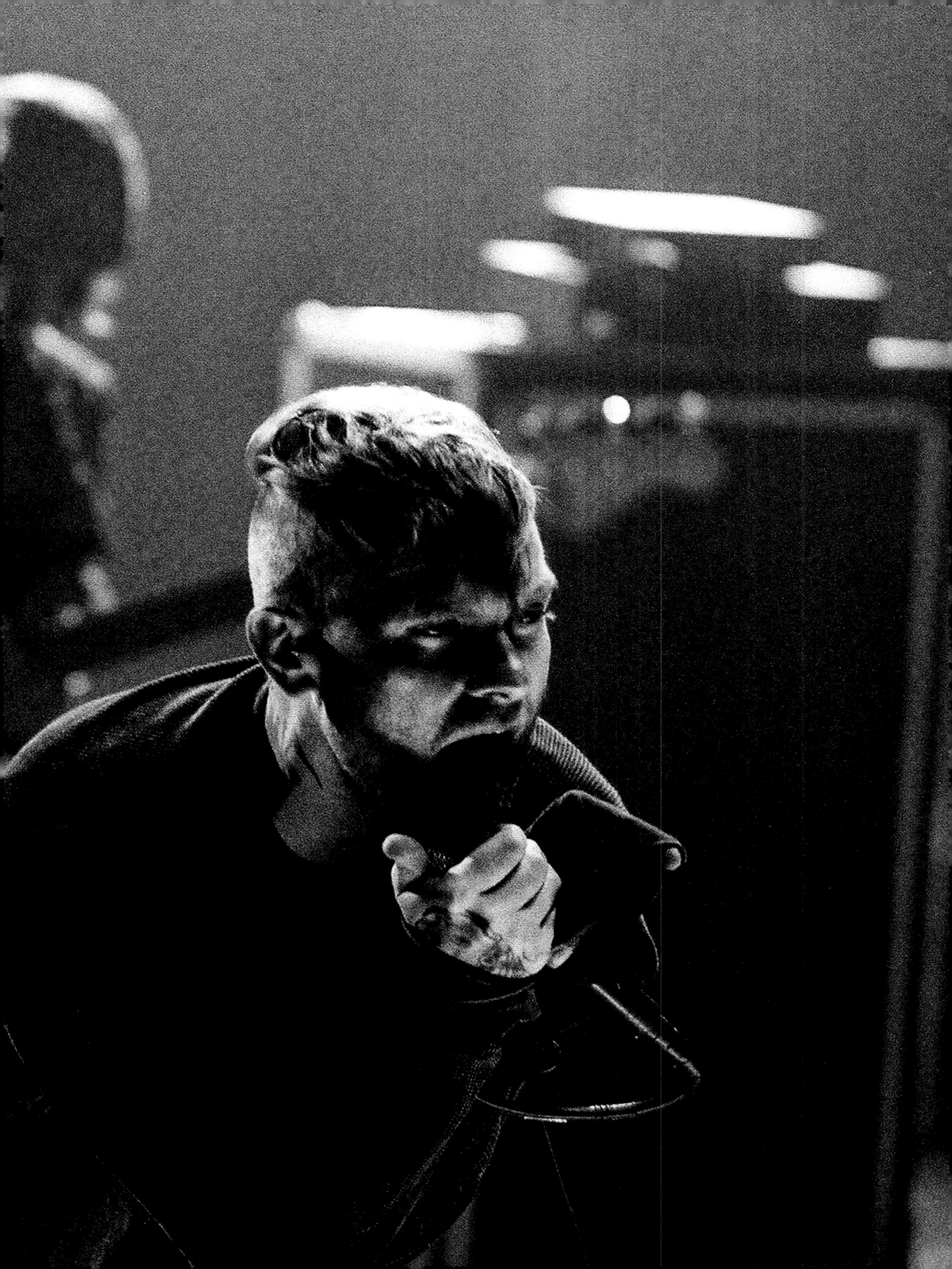

Maybe i could be the only one
who could leave her
SO I LIVE AND JUST PRETEND that i
couldn't kill her

you turning feods making other
people feel sober
and over and over

im lying to myself and this dagger's
my excuse
im a pawn i should have paid up
and i left an hour late i was laid up
i must abuse myself
im against all that i've made up
set in stone the sun will come
and i hate the light
you know i hate light

I must have caught something
in the heat of all those dances
im a worm with no more chances
and ive lost all doubt
in a chemic romance
i cant stop itching at tarnished
thoughts of hope
kinda funny lonely feeling
im in love
im not in you know its not love.

BROTHER & sisters im right
here with you
And everyones got one
a story to kill me
and im so apathetic in my resent
ment. this living and loving and
take my hand/life. knowing and not.

it like Monday to me yet My baby My baby take my baby away

00000

To me it looks So PRETTY BURNING

(v1) when i stopped to call you my little girl
i meant more so much more
than i'd like to fuck you half to death
they want to they want to
work on turning heads and breaking necks
a passtime a meantime
see their jaws drop as you fly like a
butterfly straight into my web
straight into my web

(ch) maybe i could be the only one who could leave her
so i lie and just pretend that i couldn't kill her

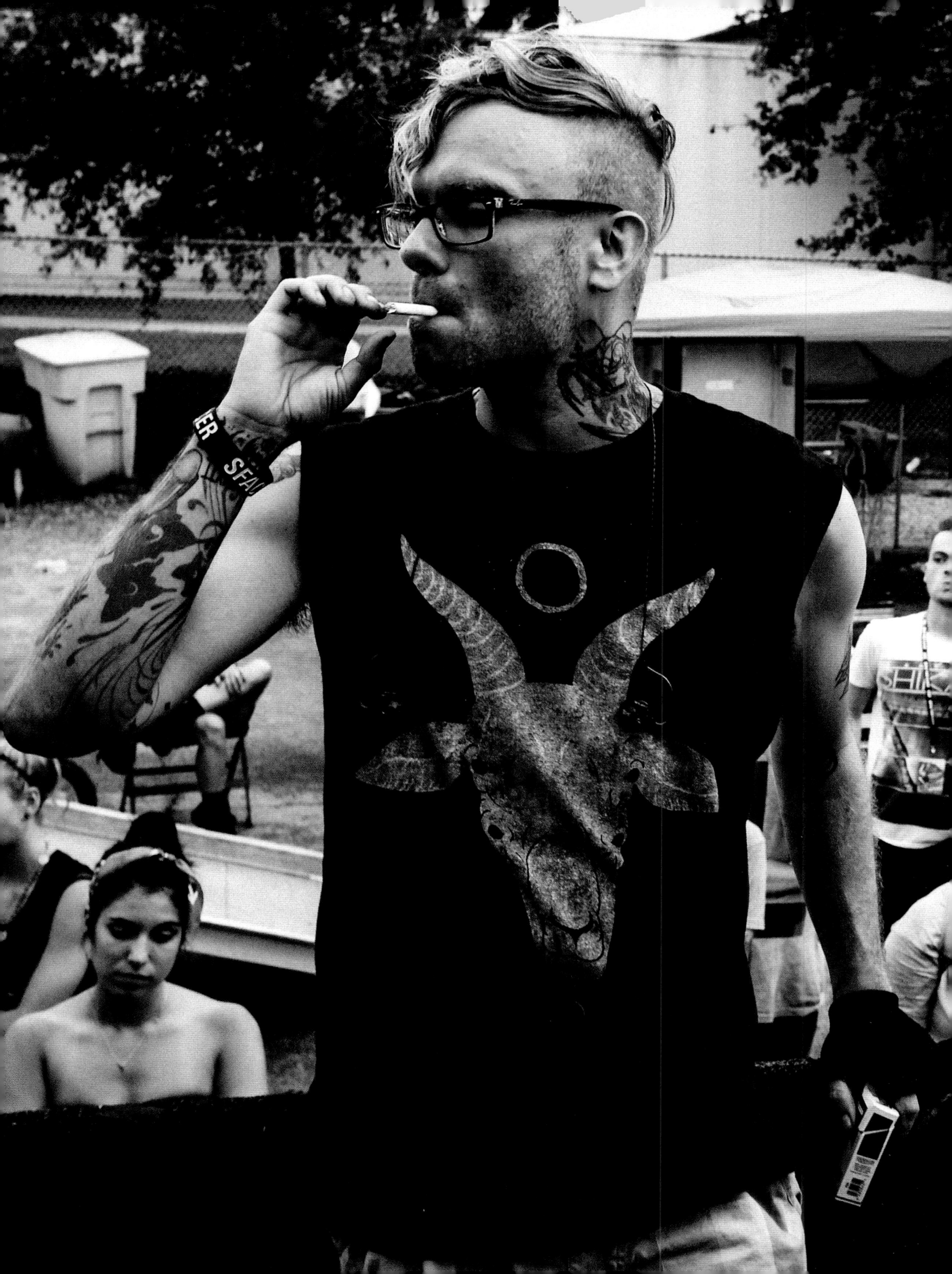

The first pass of lyrics for the song "Listening." They're quite rambling. This is a small example of how lyrics build and grow. The first pass of this song, there's only about three lines taken from the past, so it shows the connection between poetry and lyrics.

The first pass of lyrics for the song "Hard To Say," pretty tragic story. About halfway through the record, the first love of my life overdosed on heroin and passed away and I wanted to quit the band. I wanted to quit the record and wallowing in my sorrow. John Feldman came to the apartment I was staying at and picked me up and took me to a studio and forced this song out of us, which was the hardest song I've ever had to write, but so glad I got it down.

can you mask a line
cut it up in time
loosing space between vallies
and try catch a vibe
make a circle square
a rectangle curb
use a smile as a noun and not
think like a verb
Really quick switch sides
spot of filtered cancer
and this room is shrinking
now you changing places
than I switched my face
and my breathing Races
when i mentioned blue.

Haven't seen him smile
un a while.

can you mask a line
cut it up for me in time
loosing space between vallies
catch a vibe
a square circle a rectangle curb
use a smile as a noun not a verb
real quick and switch sides
spotted uniform cancer that filtered
this room is shrinking and growing
your changing places
switching faces   my breathing
kill/smile/ cut it up for me this time.
smile smile its been a while.

can
FAT A
SPOON

when the shirt came off
it was all in time
when a m-m-m- minuet turned
into a mile
than i broke that ~~smile~~ grin
and i cut it ~~up~~ out ~~turned~~
~~and~~ and you got all ~~dolled~~ ~~teared~~
on ~~up~~ by the taste of the ~~blood~~ RIVER
when you mentioned blue
all i thought was color
when you mentioned drugs
all i thought was sober
when the pants came off
~~turned me~~ ~~on~~ ~~when you turned over~~ me over
when you mentioned blue.

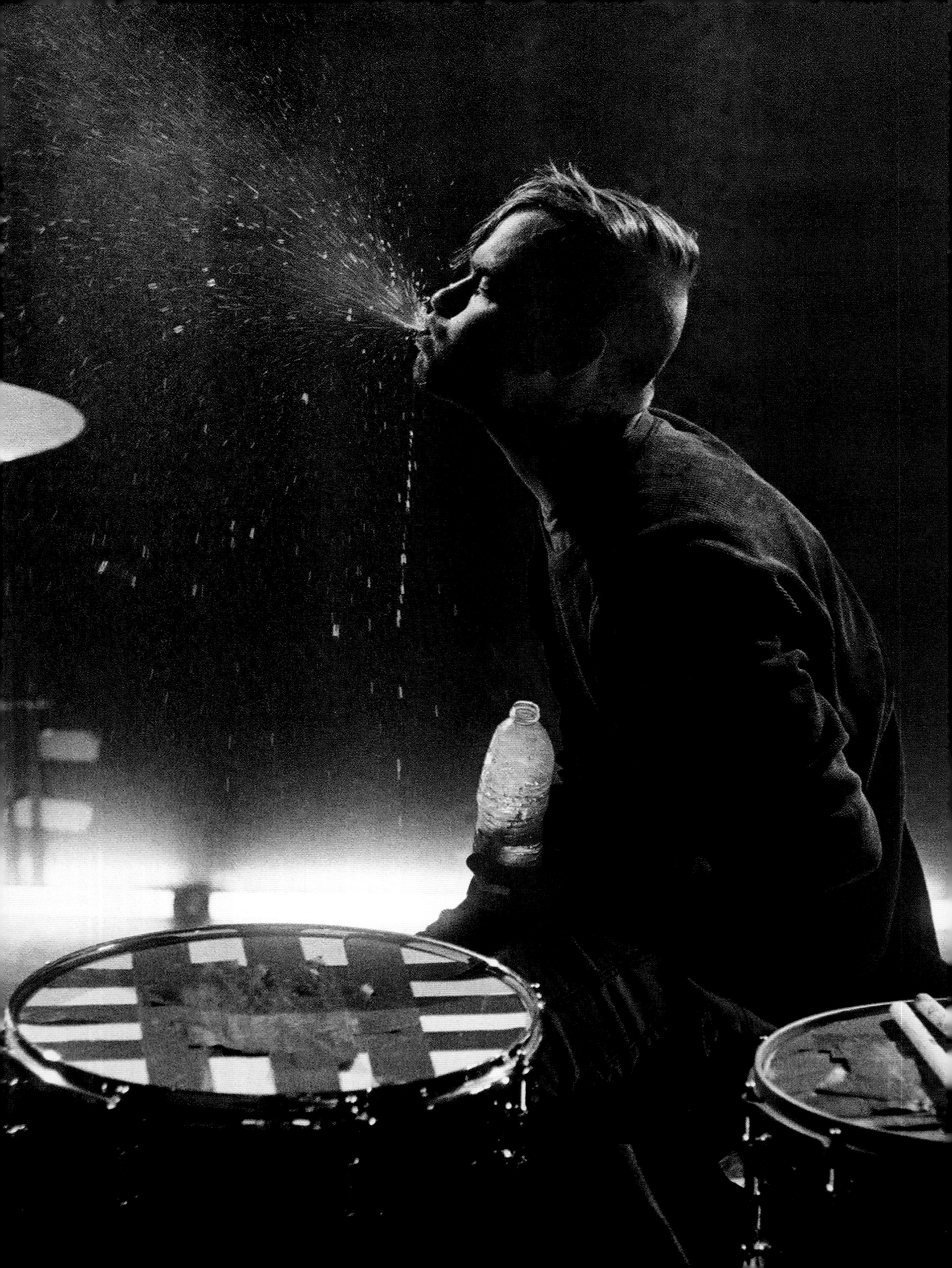

its only up or down from here kid

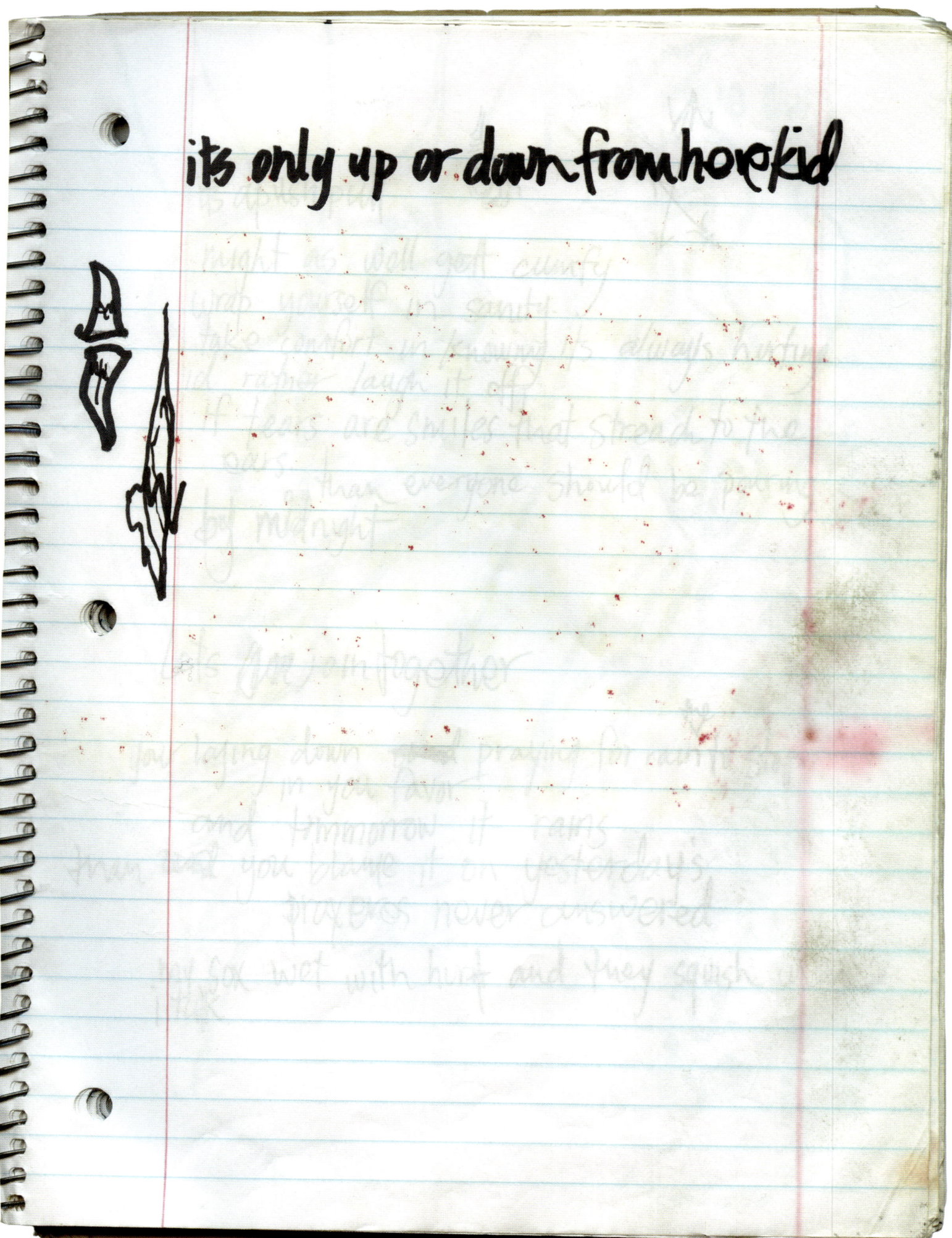

might as well get comfy
wrap yourself in sanity
take comfort in knowing its always hurting
i'd rather laugh it off
if tears are smiles that spread to the
ears
than everyone should be passing out
by midnight

lets one jam together

you laying down and praying for each day
in your favor
and tomorrow it rains
than will you blame it on yesterday's
prayers never answered
my eyes wet with hurt and they squish

its a push pull
might as well get cumfy
wrap yourself in sanity.
take comfort in knowing its always hurting
id rather laugh it off
if tears are smiles that streach to the
ears. than everyone should be pouring
by midnight

Lets love join together

your laying down and praying for rain to stop
in you favor
and timmorrow it rains
than and you blame it on yesterday's
prayeres never answered

my sox wet with hurt and they squish when
i talk

The lyrics for "I'm a Fake," also written outside the studio in my car, which was the normal place. My creative peak hours are from eleven at night until five in the morning. I think that every artist struggles with this idea of imposter syndrome and I think that this is my ode to my own imposter syndrome. I'm a fake and it really sums it up.

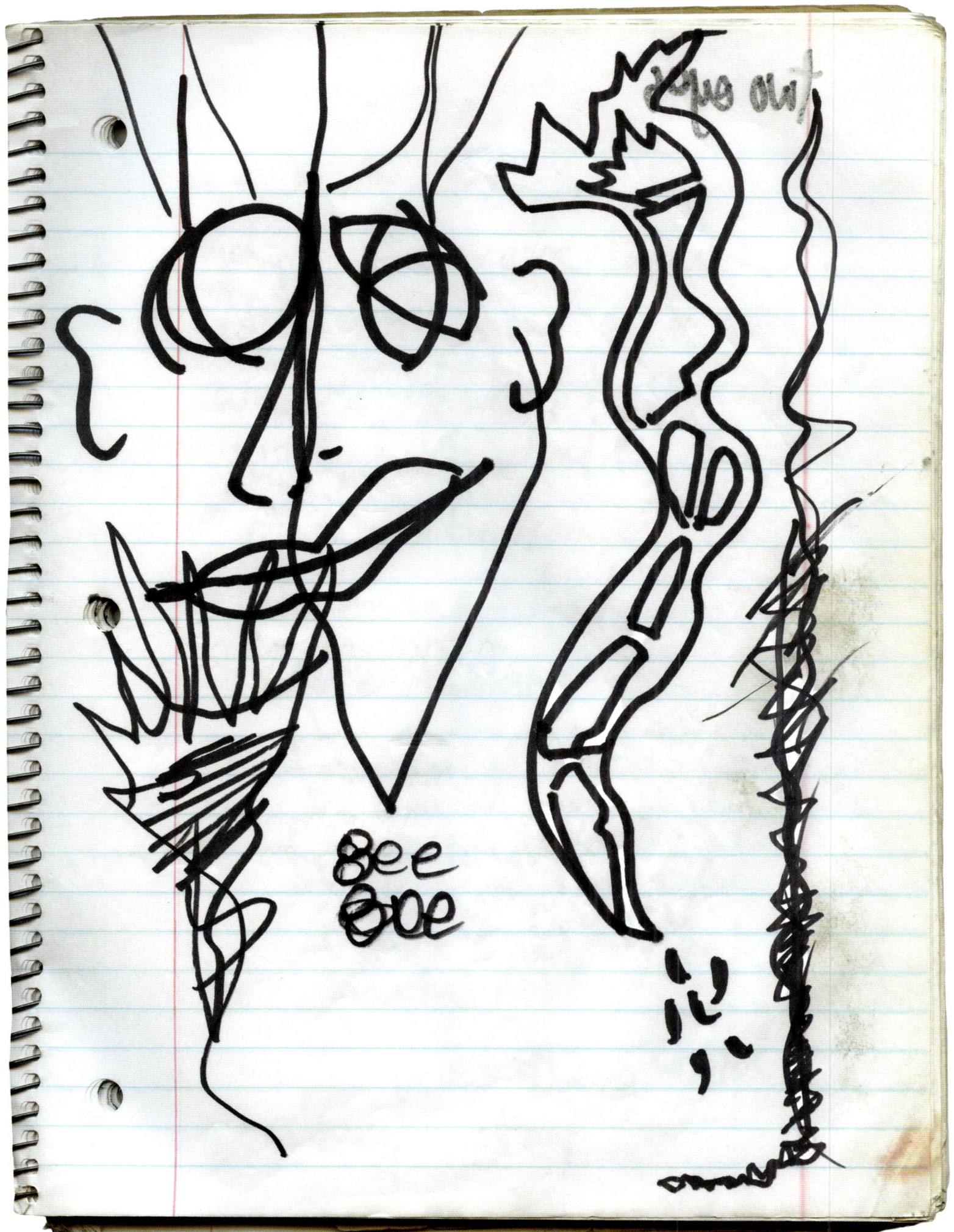

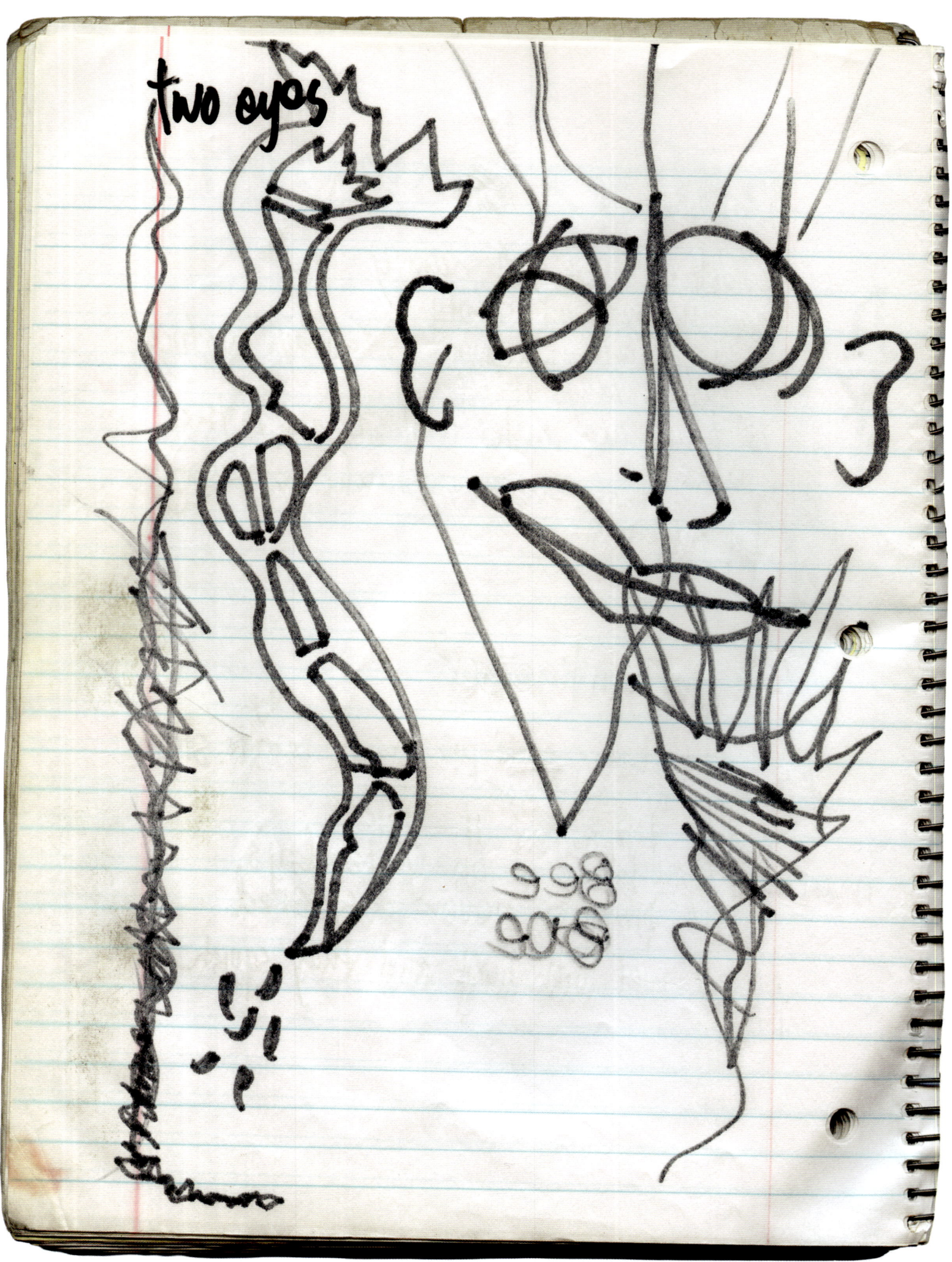

two eyes

when we were in Japan
After every show
we would play this
Well, bob would
and mufuden
Japanese kids
were fucking
freaking out
they like
had a dance
party
no they would
alway stay

we all want a crush that ~~stays~~ could stay.
like this little girl her wanting
my giving (thats backwards)
this bleeding positivity
infected i caught what i deserved
I just want to touch your face
eat those words that ive wasted
and taste you.
Just held ~~gup~~ on a shelf in a case
words are webs and this spiders amazing
but im ~~trying~~ to give not to take
although some of my strikes wont erase
I know all of my dreams worth the chase

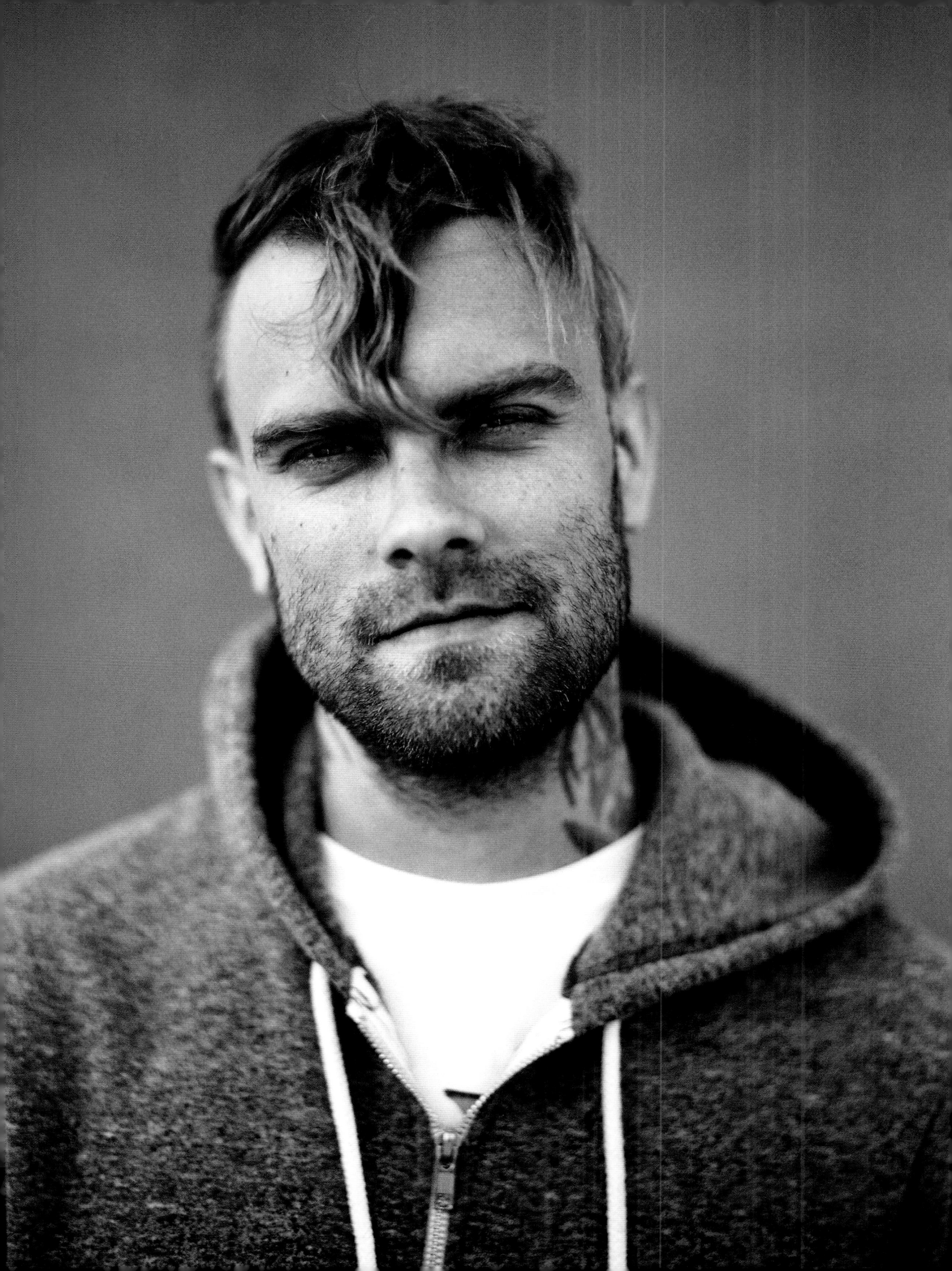

we all want a crush that could stay.
like this little girl, her wanting, my giving (thats backwards)
I just want to touch your face.
eat those words that i've wasted and taste you.
just held up on a shelf in a case
words are webs and this spiders amazing.
But I'm trying to give not to take
i've been digging a hole with your name on it

you can keep the words-keep the words-shit

? cause yesterday little cupid got shot down?

blank and   shooting
    blank   blanks
          mind   shooting-
          blanks
          cant
          even

cant
even
masterbate

The song "Take It Away" also has heavy connotations to my lyrical upbringing as far as my religious background as well. Then there's me trying to formulate lyrics for the song "Sound Effects and Over Dramatics." I got deathly ill with the flu, and I remember going out that night right on the beach recording the song on the rocks right in front of the beach. It was a memory that I'll never forget being sick as a dog. You could still hear the beach in the recording of the song as well.

you looked so stuck
so sad I had
to **make you**

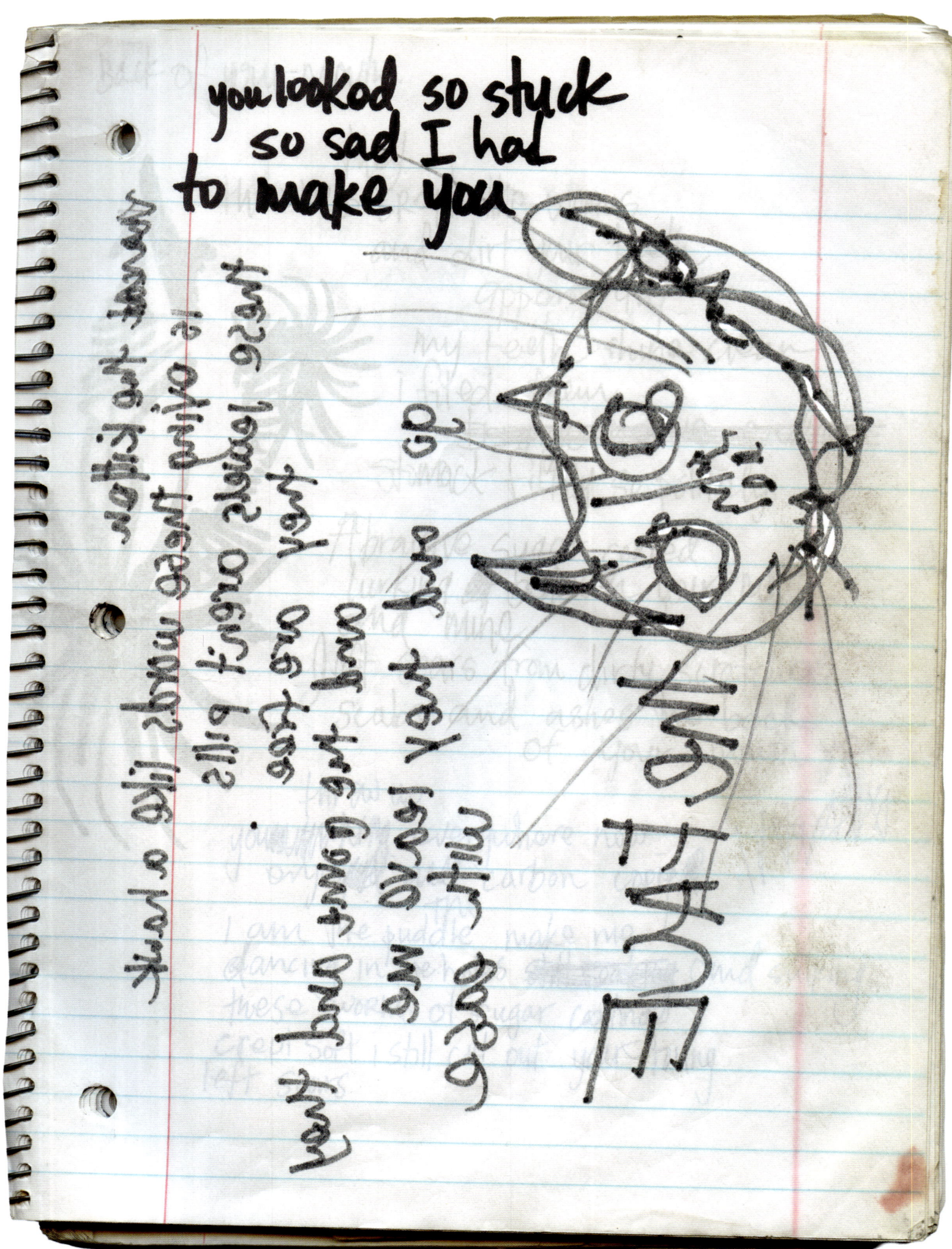

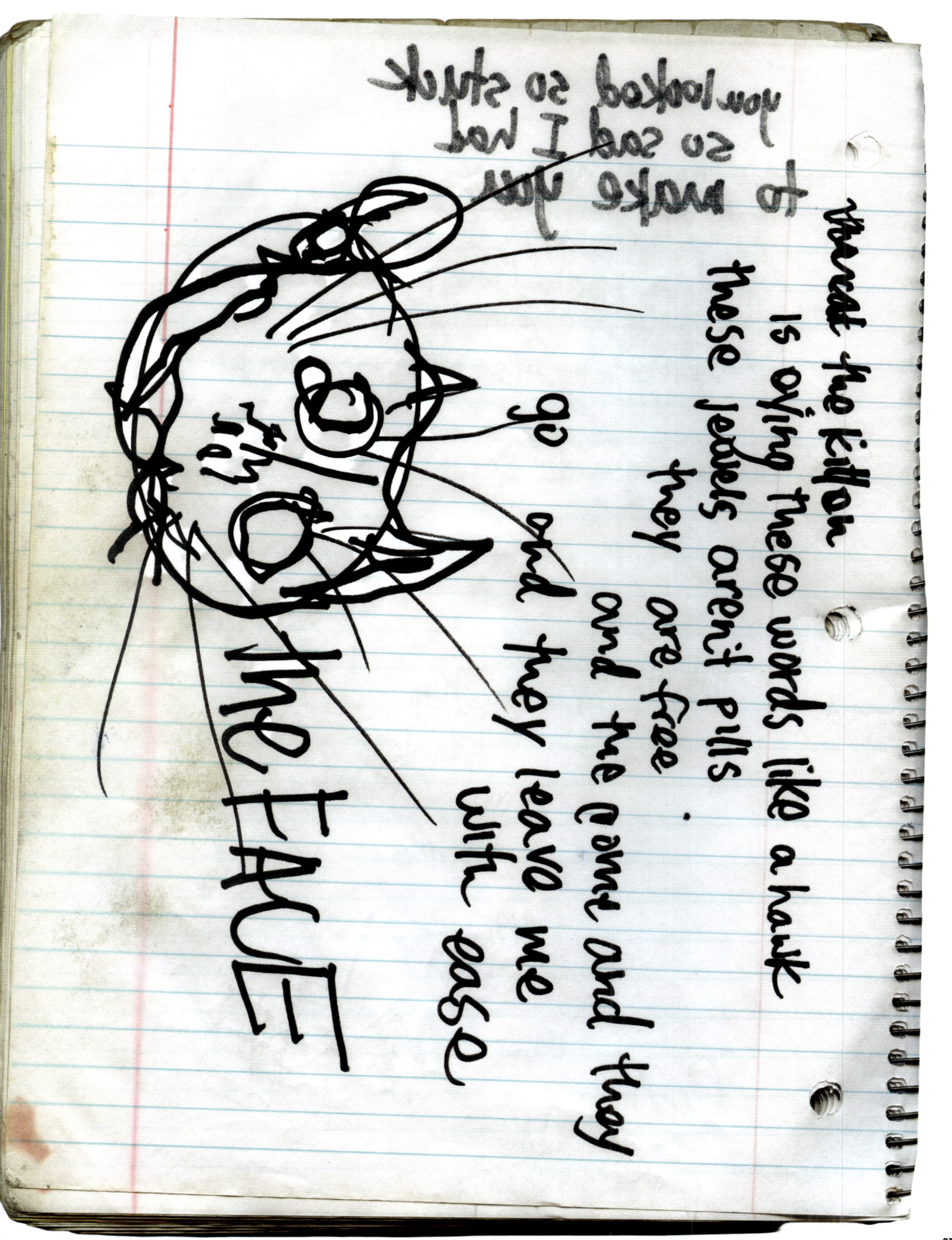

threat the kitten
is crying these words like a hawk
these jewels aren't pills
they are free
and the come and they
go and they leave me
with ease

THE FACE

Back of your mouth.

they
the words crept like worms
and dirt your teeth
apparently
my teeth shine clean
i filed them
~~i made more cushs~~
stomach filthy so politely.

Abraisive sugar coated
lurking at between your mouth
and mine.
left scars from dirty scratches
scabs and ashes the back
of your mouth yea.

threw up
you ~~fucking~~ everywhere now.
on you ~~and~~ and carbon copies

the
I am the puddle make me
dancing in the holes ~~still soaking~~ and sulking
these worms of sugar coating
crept soft i still cut out your young
left scars

maybe i could be the only one
that could leave her.
should i cry to think that when
i left it just killed her.

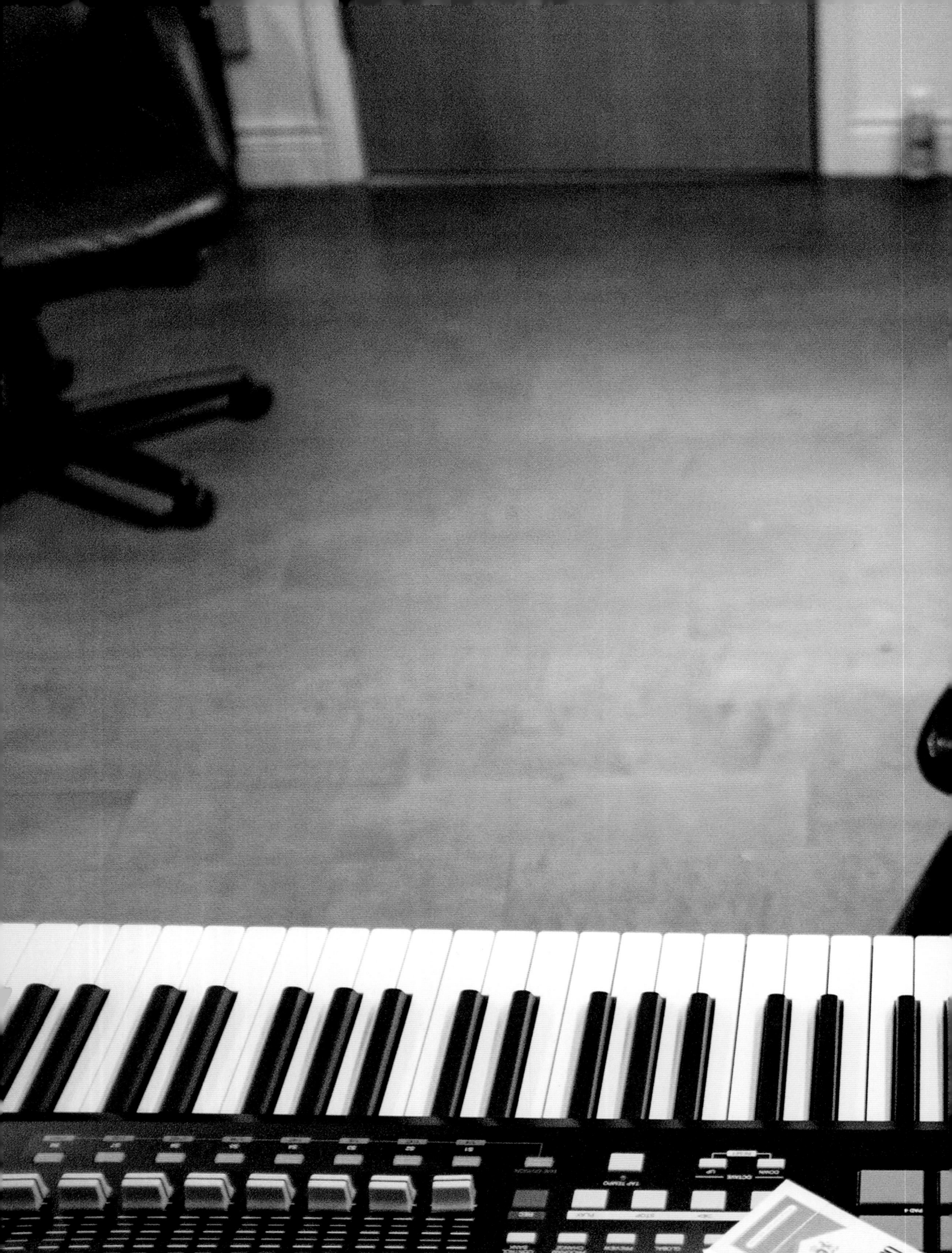

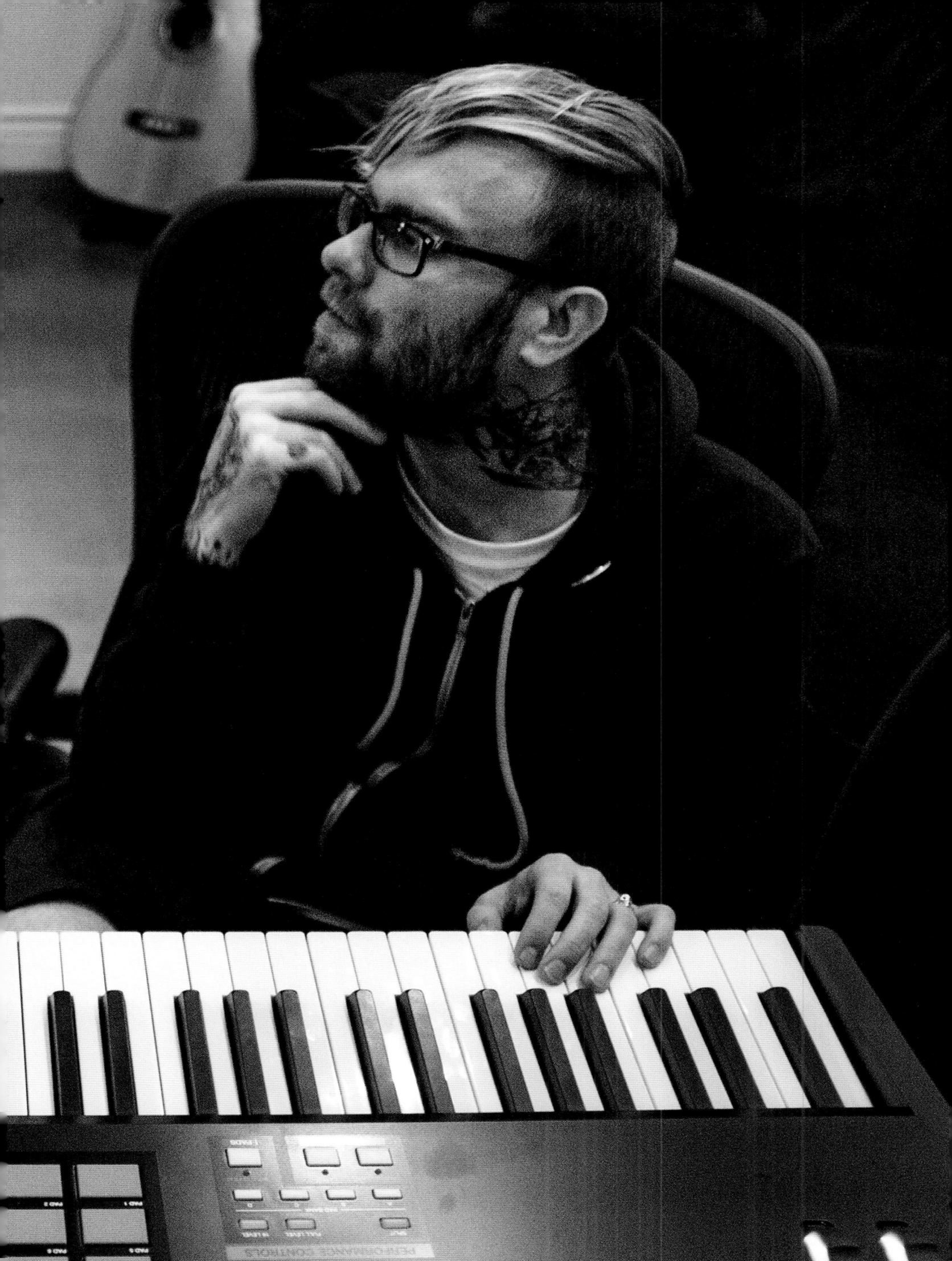

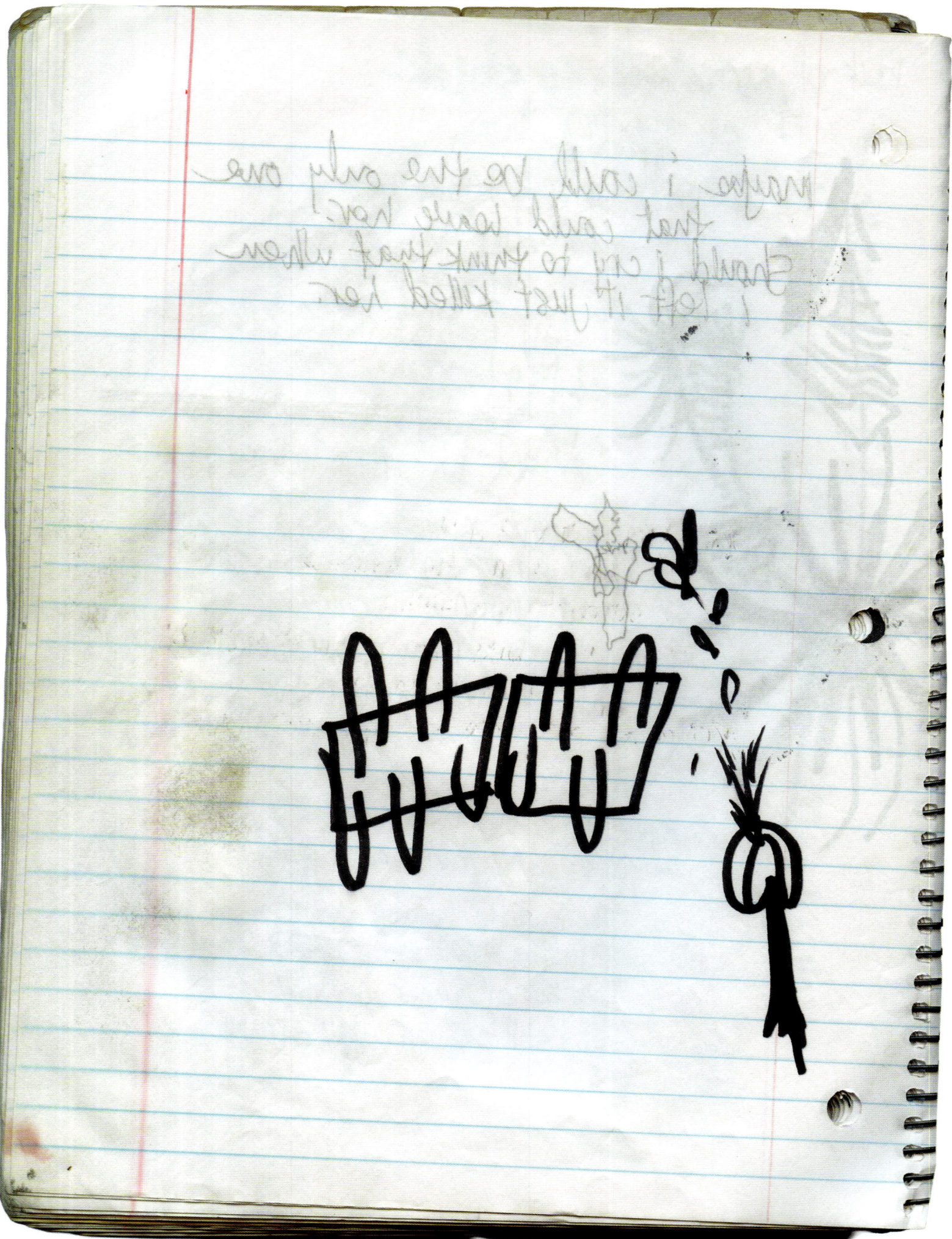

the warm of the sun on my back
not inspirering
listening warting remembering
    ever hero that ever failed
me

Jess
323

the warm of the gun
    sing praise to the heavens
worried songs from a sinner
    coughing chunks of cracked melody
to offer up to nothing
this balled of doubtful agravation

There were a bunch of songs in this journal that
didn't make the record, and they all made this
B-sides record called *Shallow Believer*, and this
is, I think the first pass at the song "Back of Your
Mouth," which is one of my favorites that didn't
make the record. When I drove back to Utah from
LA to visit my family. And on the way I stopped
by my friend Sarah's house and she was on crystal
meth. We had a big long night, and this page
definitely represents a time in my youth where I
was free to do whatever was there, although I did
not do meth that night

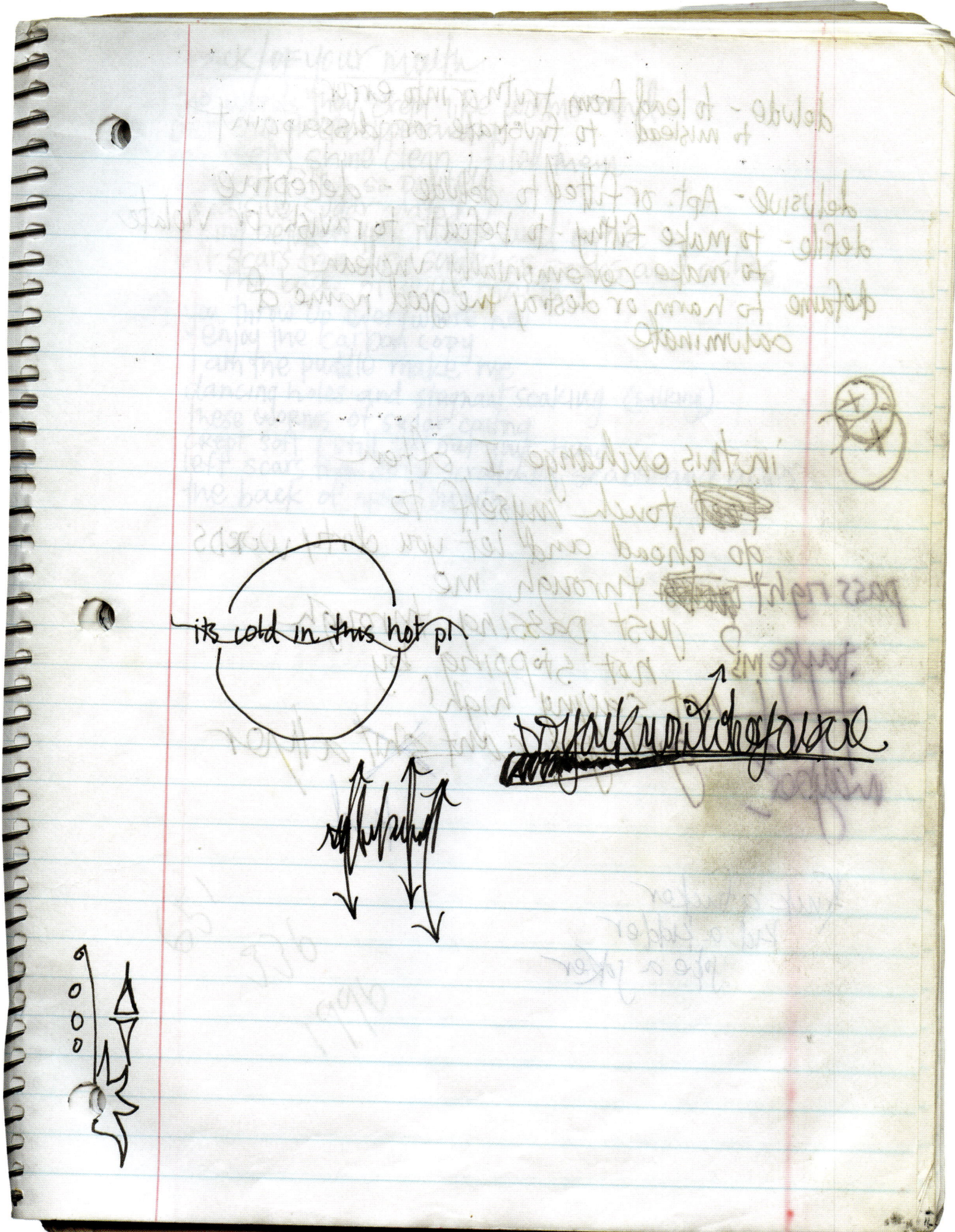

its cold in this hot pl

delude - to lead from truth or into error
  to mislead to frustrate or dissapoint

delusive - Apt. or fitted to delude - deceptive
defile - to make filthy - to befoul - to ravish or violate
  to make ceremonially unclean
defame to harm or destroy the good name of
calumniate

in this exchange I often
~~feel~~ touch myself to
go ahead and let you dirty words
pass right ~~~~ through me
  just passing through
not stopping by
not saying high!
girl you cant ~~shit~~ all ~~yor~~
    kid

pause m?

maybe

fuck a fucker
kid a kidder
joke a joker

BACK/OF your mouth

(v1) the words they crept like worms and
dirt your teeth apperantly
my teeth shine clean i filed them
stomach filthy so politely,
Abraisive sugar coated
lurking between your mouth and mine
left scars from dirty scratches scabs and ashes
　　　the back of your mouth

(v2) you throw up everywhere now
enjoy the karbon copy
i am the puddle make me
dancing holes and stagnant soaking (sulking)
these worms of sugar coating
crept soft i still cut out your toung
left scars from dirty scratches scabs and ashes
the back of your mouth

651

sleeping bags
with digital color
black with trust
reinforcing pain or something yeah
something hahaha lol brb g2g

i never need to take a day off
from myself

even thought I want to take a
day off from
the rest

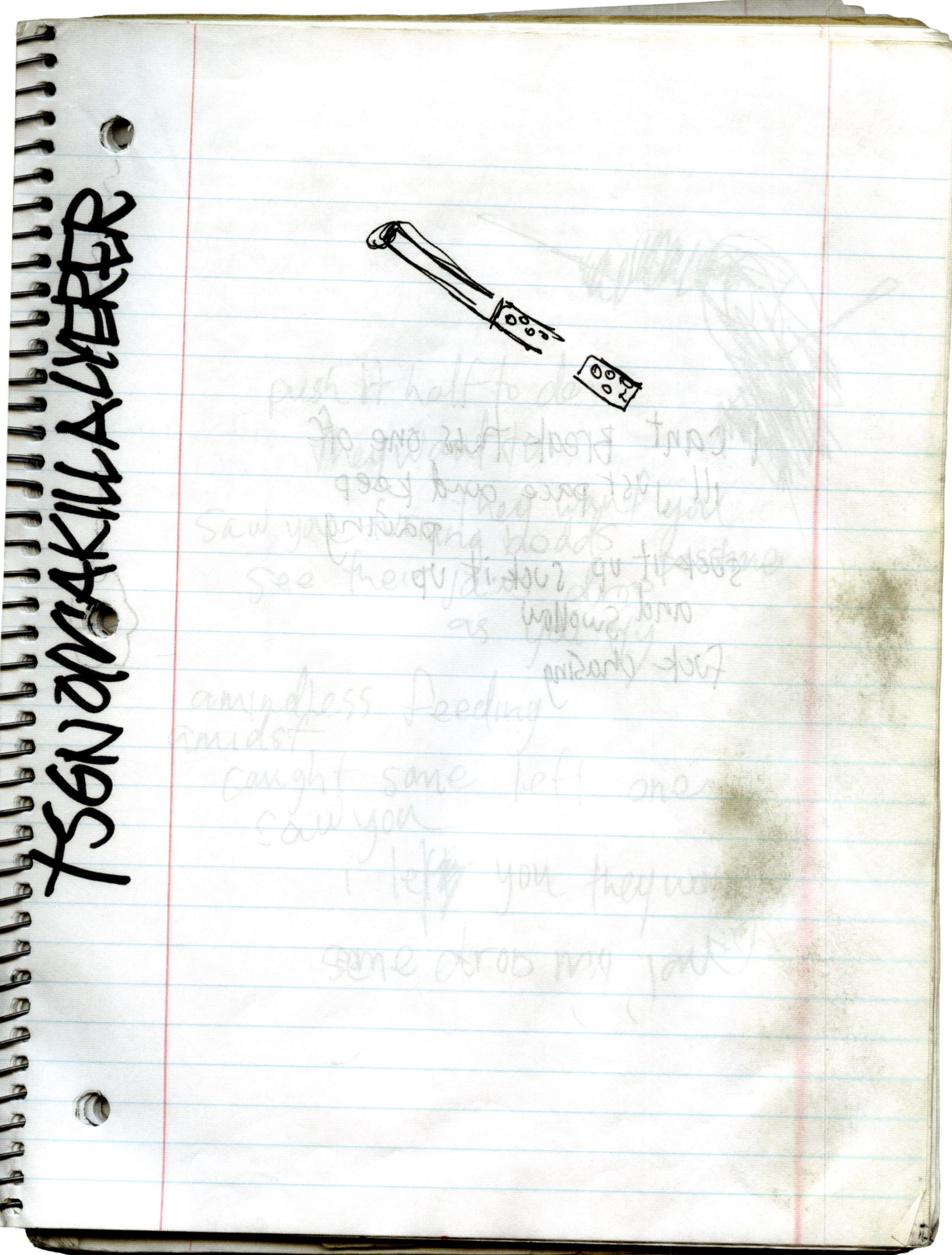

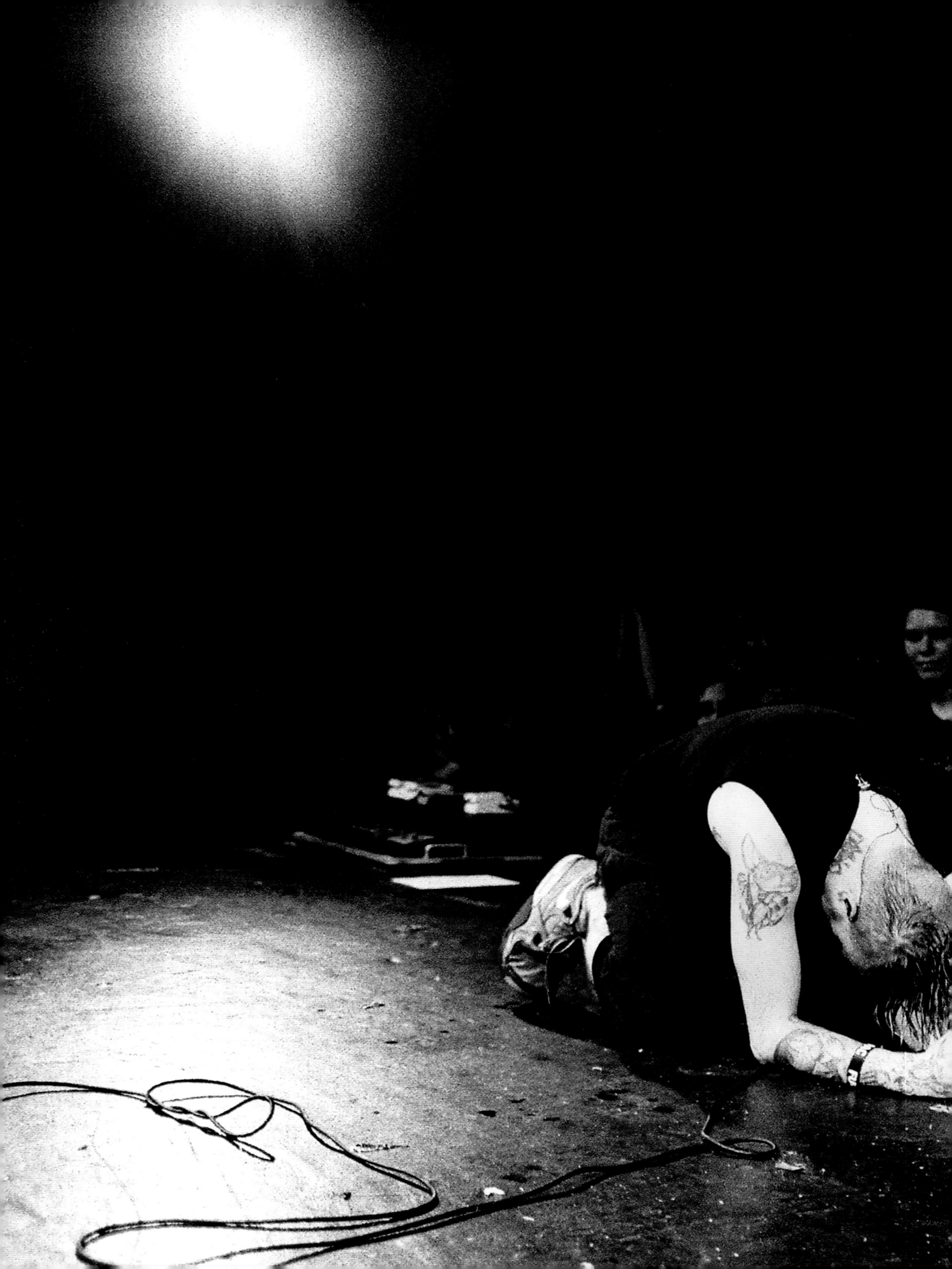

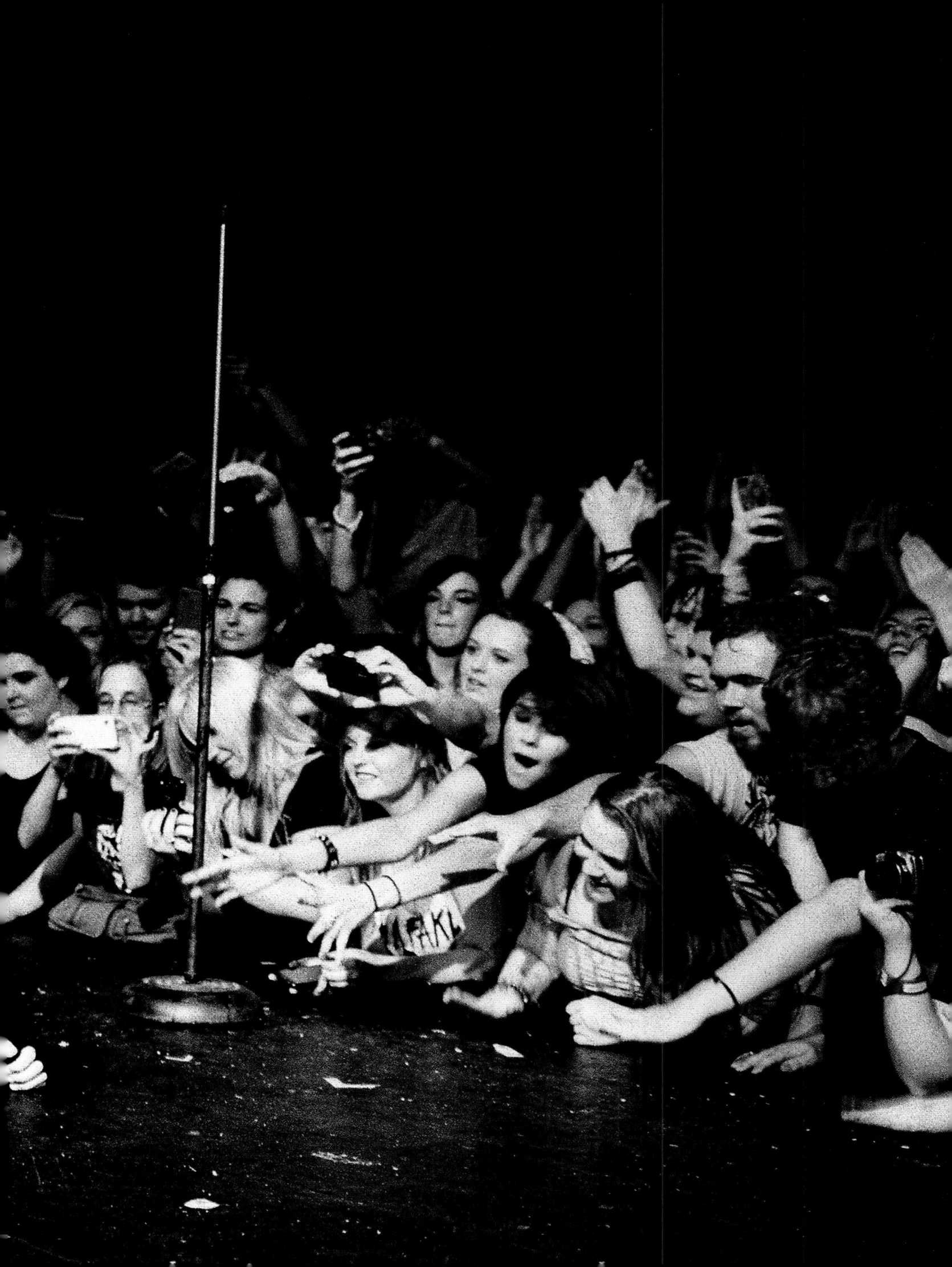

There's also the only pass for the lyrics of
"Yesterday's Feelings." There was a lot of
time in the recording process for this record
that the band was getting along really well
and jamming out in the living room of our
apartment, and Quinn had his acoustic
guitar and this song just felt like it came
out of nowhere and was finished within 10
minutes. One of those magic moments with
songwriting, great songs you usually, I find
come that way. Don't have to think too much
about 'em. They just kind of come out of you.

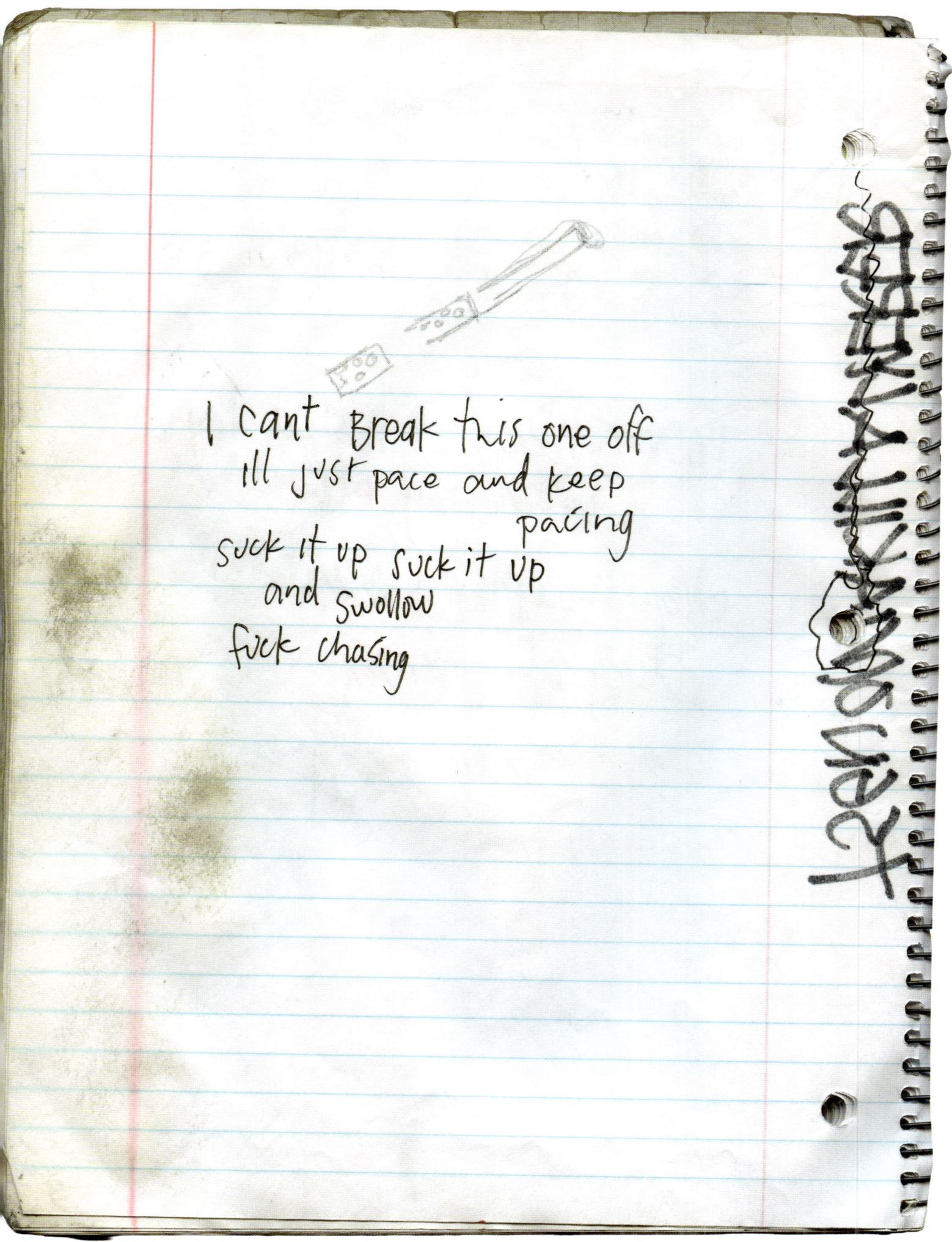

I cant break this one off
ill just pace and keep
                    pacing
suck it up suck it up
and swollow
fuck chasing

push it half to de
they want to
saw you turning bloods they want you
see their jaws drop passtime
as you fly

amindless feeding
amidst
caught some left one
saw you
i left you they want to

some drop my jaw

smeared ink in cursive you think we all got left behind
.the more we sink and pretend to own are own selves
in moving in sound effects and over dramatics,
not really a groove but a chunk of movement
the way the pen moves the ink i remember what its
like to not move if i had any enemys they would
surely be on my list now. and these are not words
just filler for my new idea money money money
the way the pen moves now with creativity
its talked about like heat rising, moving not
in a cliche but sinking to the pit of my guts
and in through and out my fingertips reaching
through foreward and backward movement

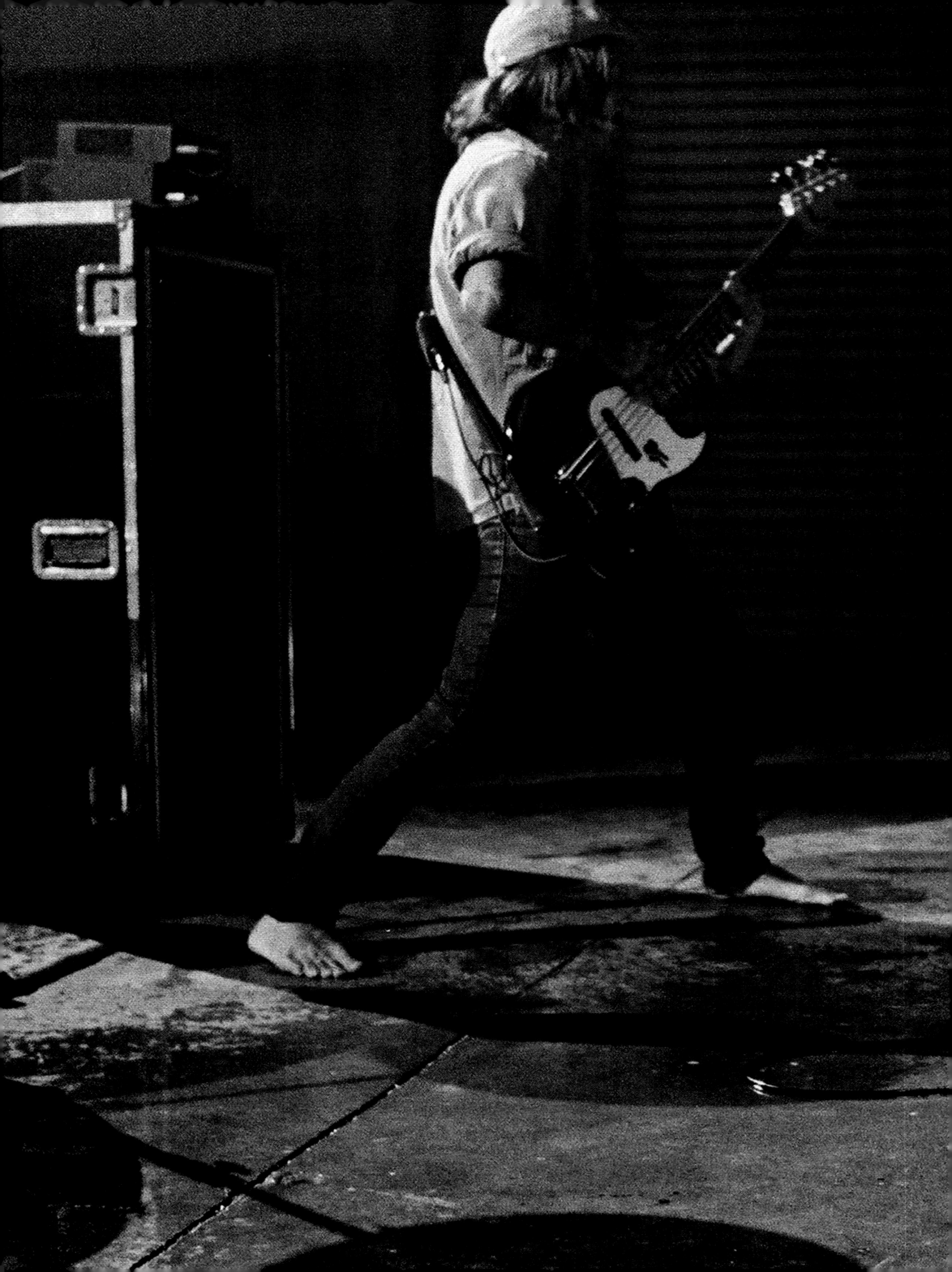

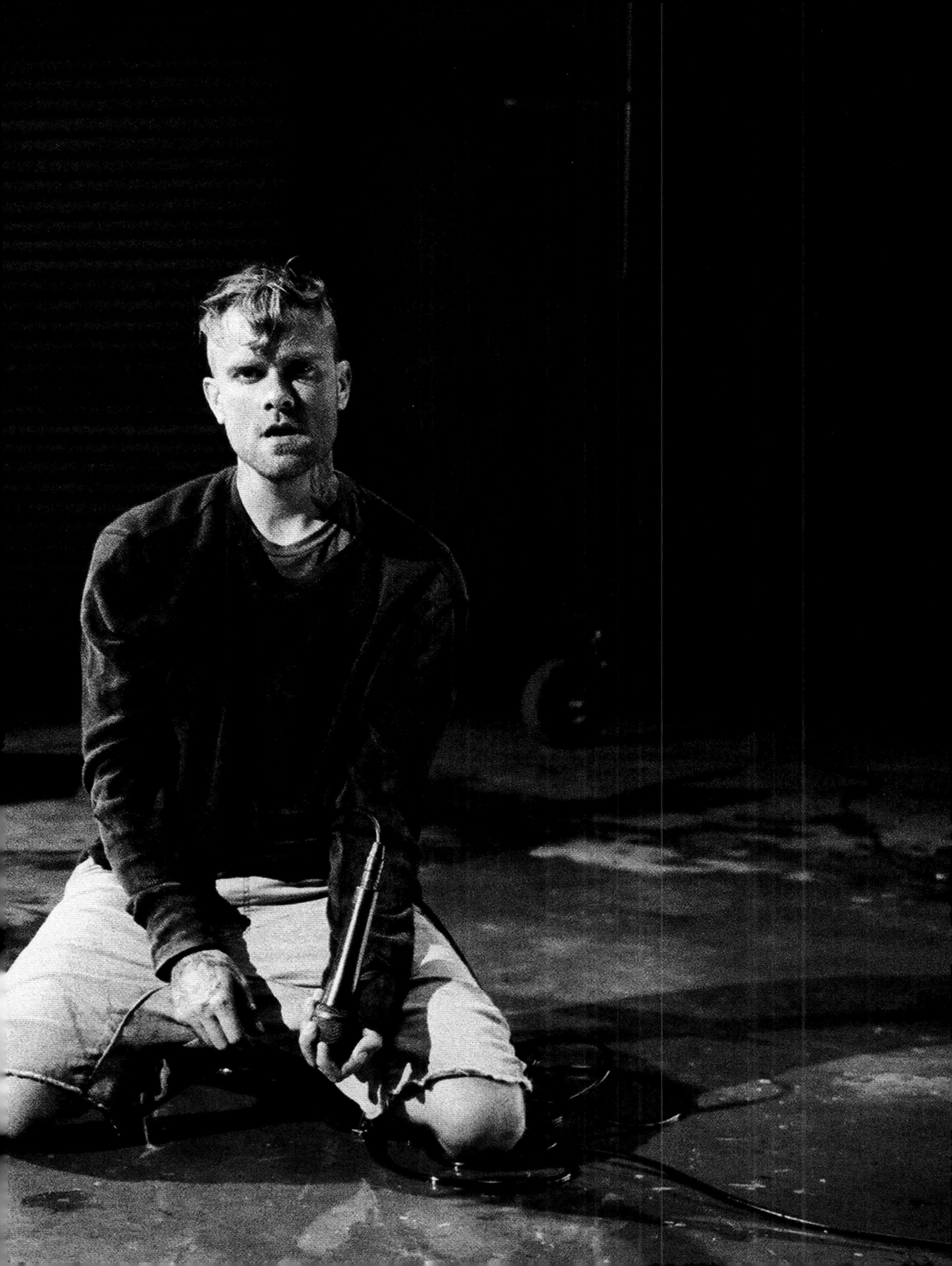

WILL I be in a bad mood
all the time when im
older?

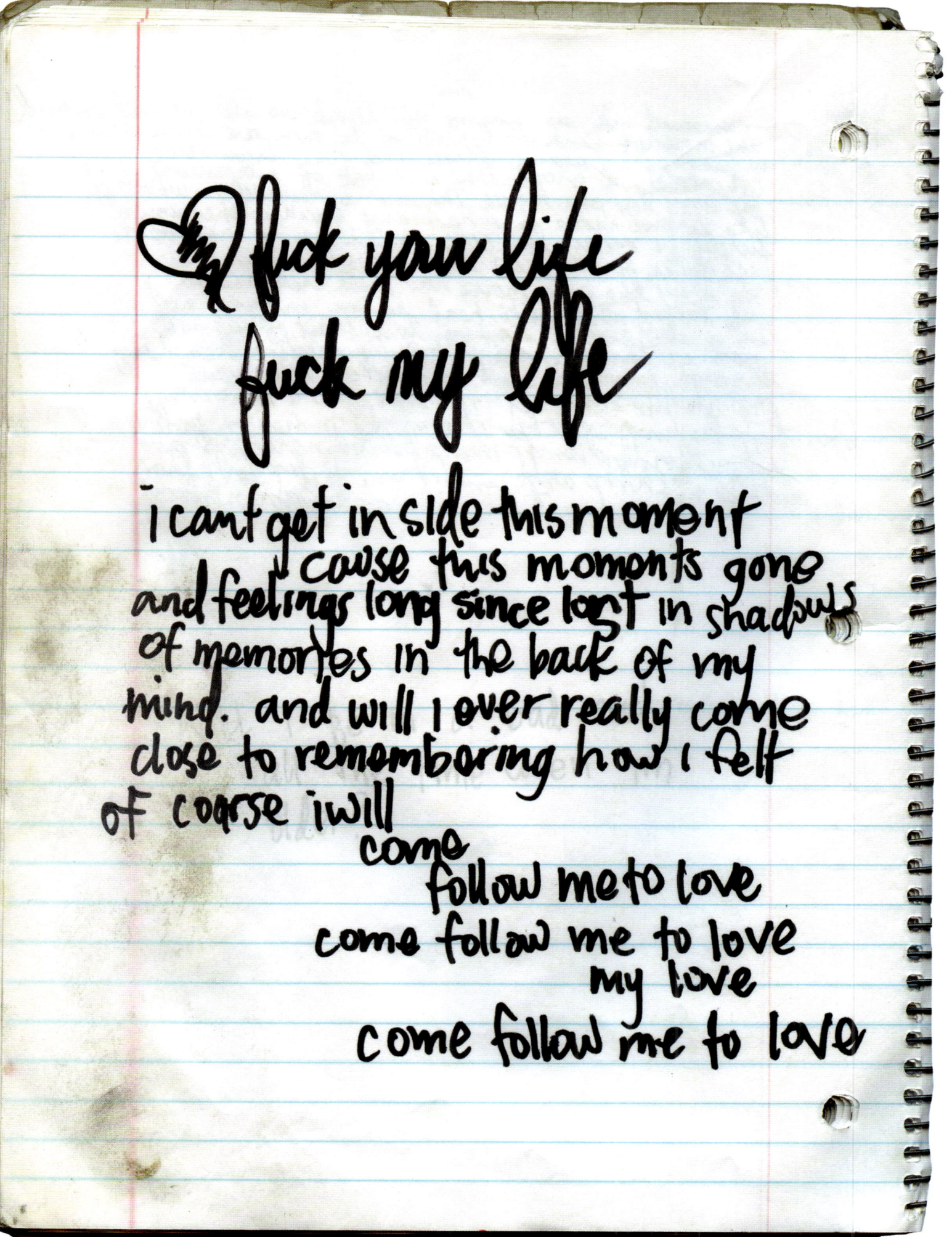

fuck your life
fuck my life

i cant get inside this moment
cause this moments gone
and feelings long since lost in shadows
of memories in the back of my
mind. and will i ever really come
close to remembering how i felt
of coarse i will
                    come
                follow me to love
            come follow me to love
                        my love
            come follow me to love

I had thought of rose pedals
perfectly pure
and the slightest
bit of pressure
would bury you alive.

i have thought of tasting the red that is in you
with what ive been givin
you'll never survive
the cold has arrived with him

i burned you cold and dead outside.

So don't i couldn't see my hand
moving never changes not
no matter how bad you might think that you want me
just your still gog going to die alone.

all?

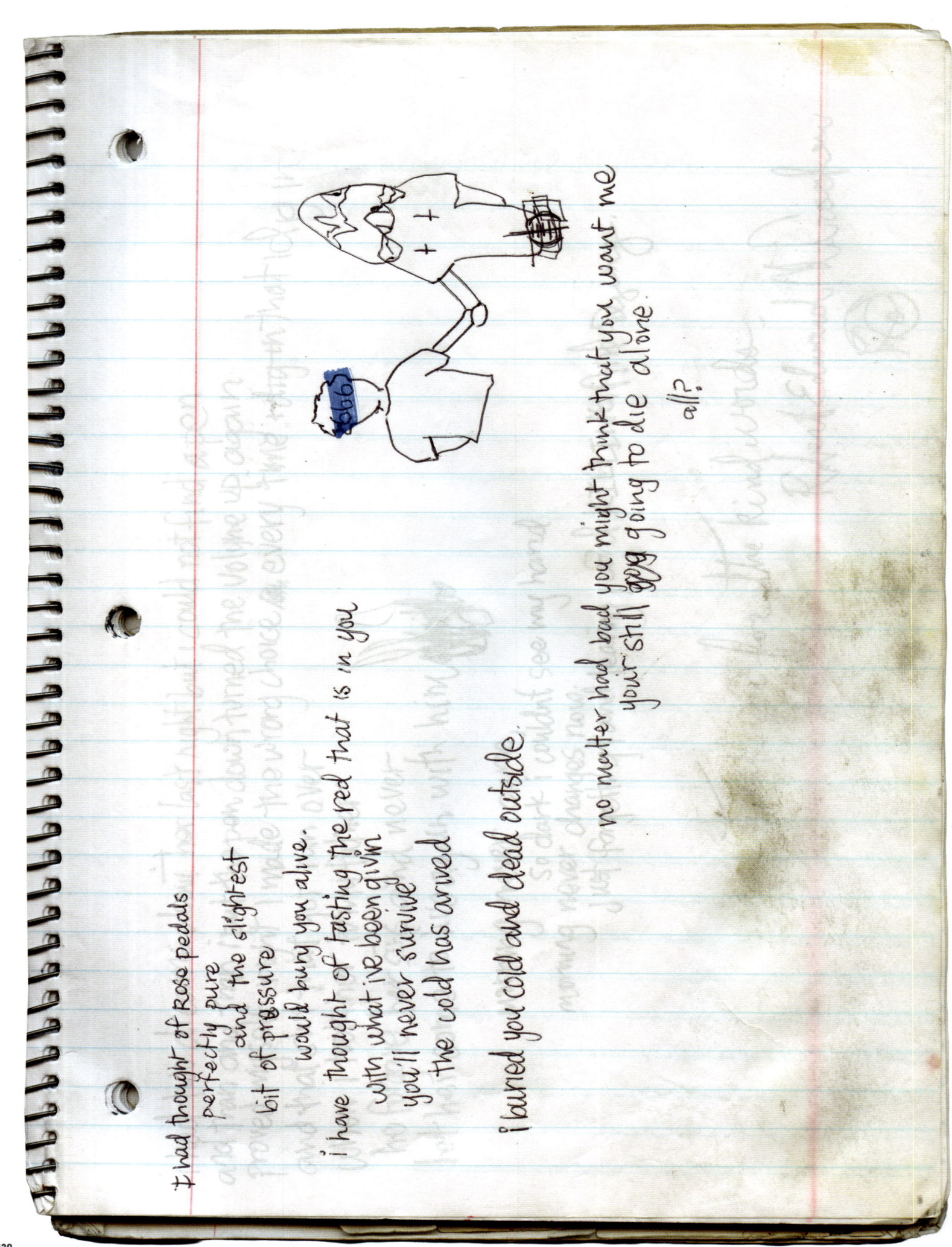

This included the first and only pass of lyrics for "Light with a Sharpened Edge." I wrote this song in my car as well about drug abuse and death, and this was before Kate passed away. I think a lot of the record had this weird, daunting foreshadowing of what I was about to experience in the next couple months, real death and real tragedy, which for me, I had never lost someone close to me before. So it was real serious.

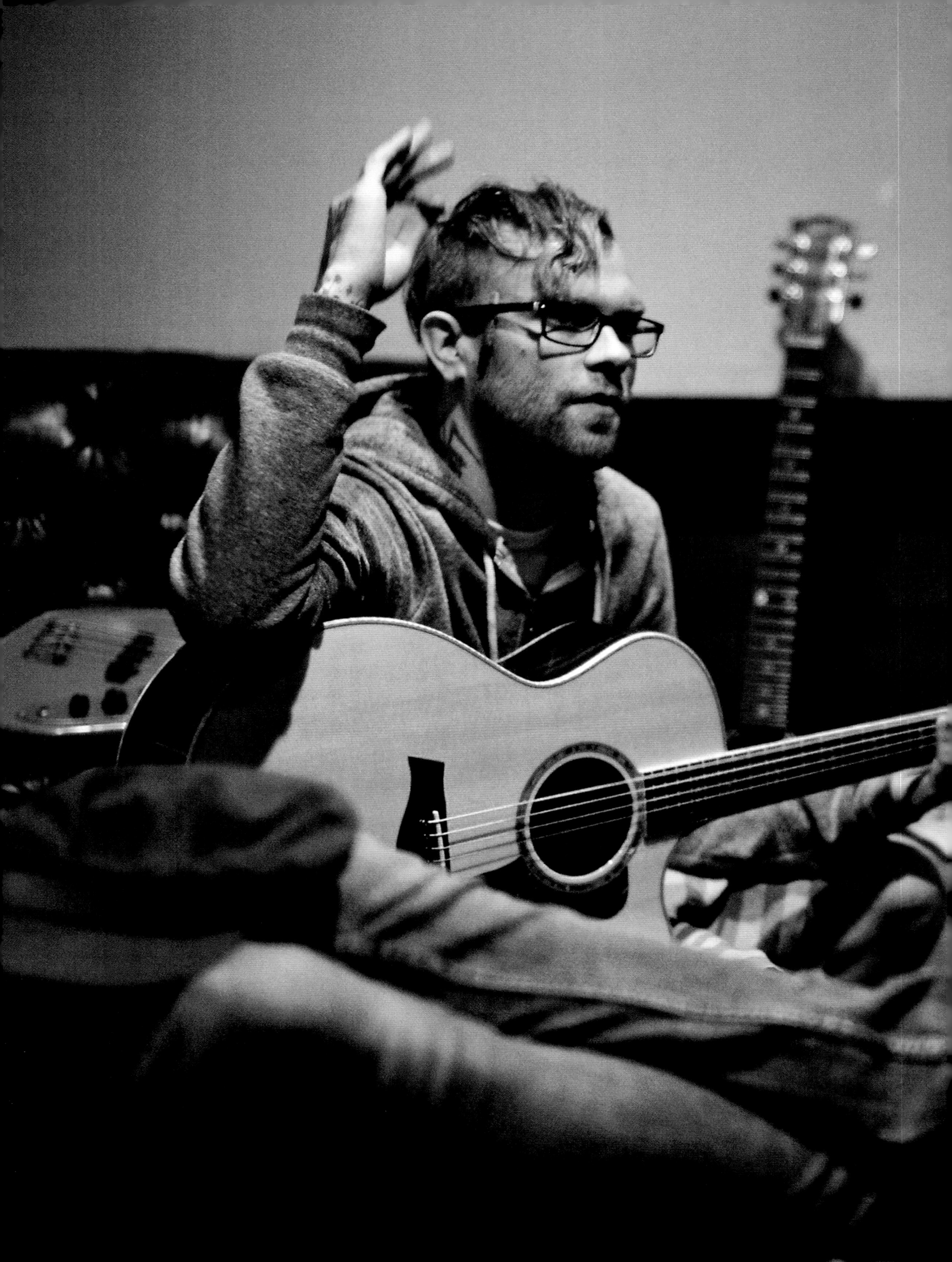

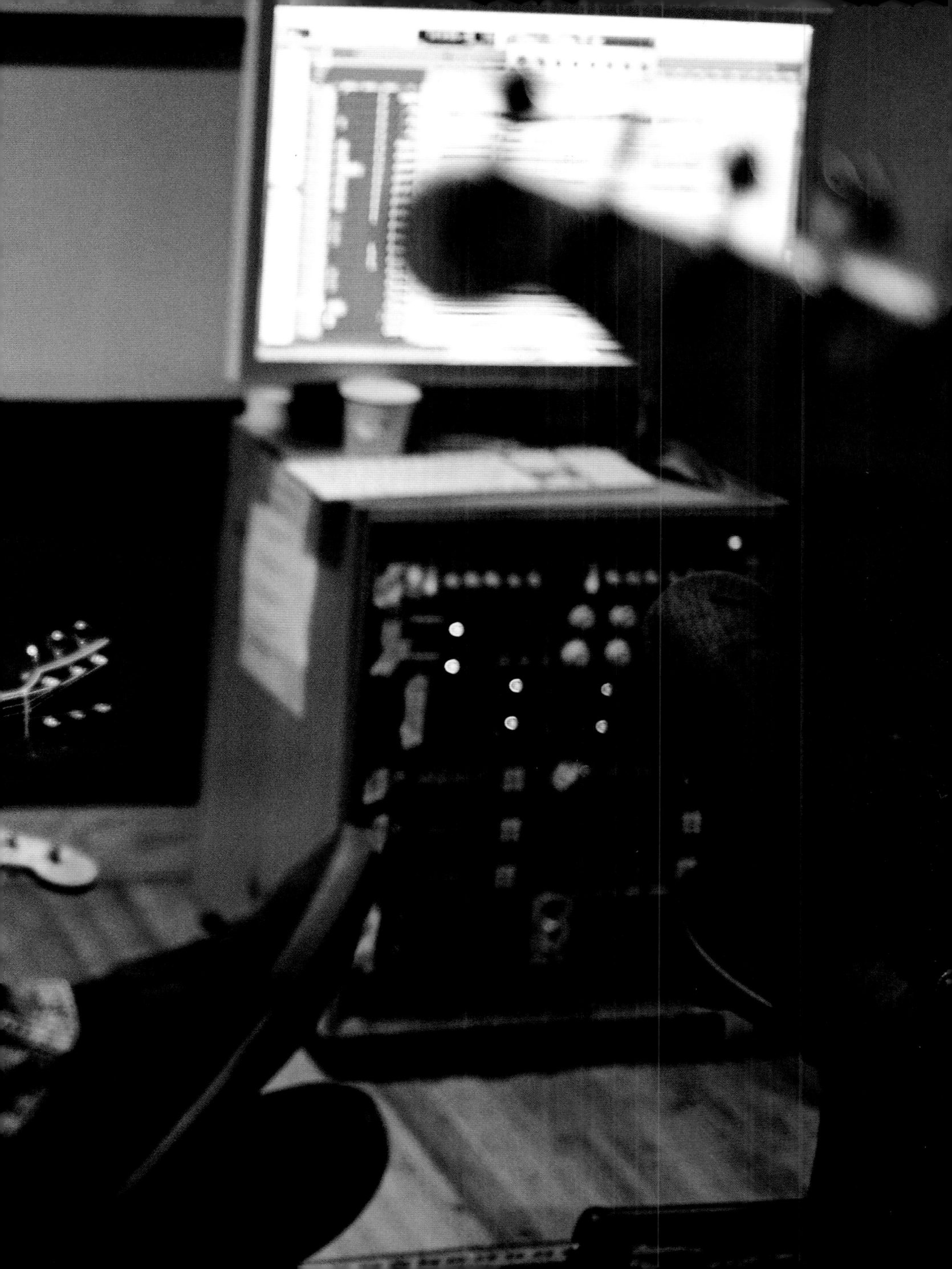

if you're not going to kill it let it live. live like me
you learnt to hate me and
every day.

i had two dreams about her last night but i could not find a pen
and than and than i but the pen down turned the volume up again
proved myself right right i made the wrong choice every time i tright that i gave in.
and that slut that got run over
when i took her my father
he forgave her sins and never
let her come to live again with him

morning never came,
So don't i couldn't see my hand
morning never changes now.
Just forgetting, and leaving, and KILLING And Dying.

Thank you for the kind words.
Robert Edward Masacesu

if your not going to kill it let it live. live like me
and learn to hate me ~~and~~
day by day

im not feeling to well
all this time ive spent healing
all my courge is here
but im still just a kitten
will the fire jumb out of its place
burn my room
or will my shoos catch on fire HOLD my FIRE
as im running away
it feels good to say that im all alone
and theres no one around (me)
i know feelings are all in my head
and i know that your dead and i hate it
thats all

i love it how you yelled and left
and ripped the heart out of my chest
and lied your face off right to death
and yes i loved your hands around my neck
you fake! loved it you fake
i really really loved it
fuck your fucking face fuck you like fuck you
fuck you you fuck face fucker FUCK

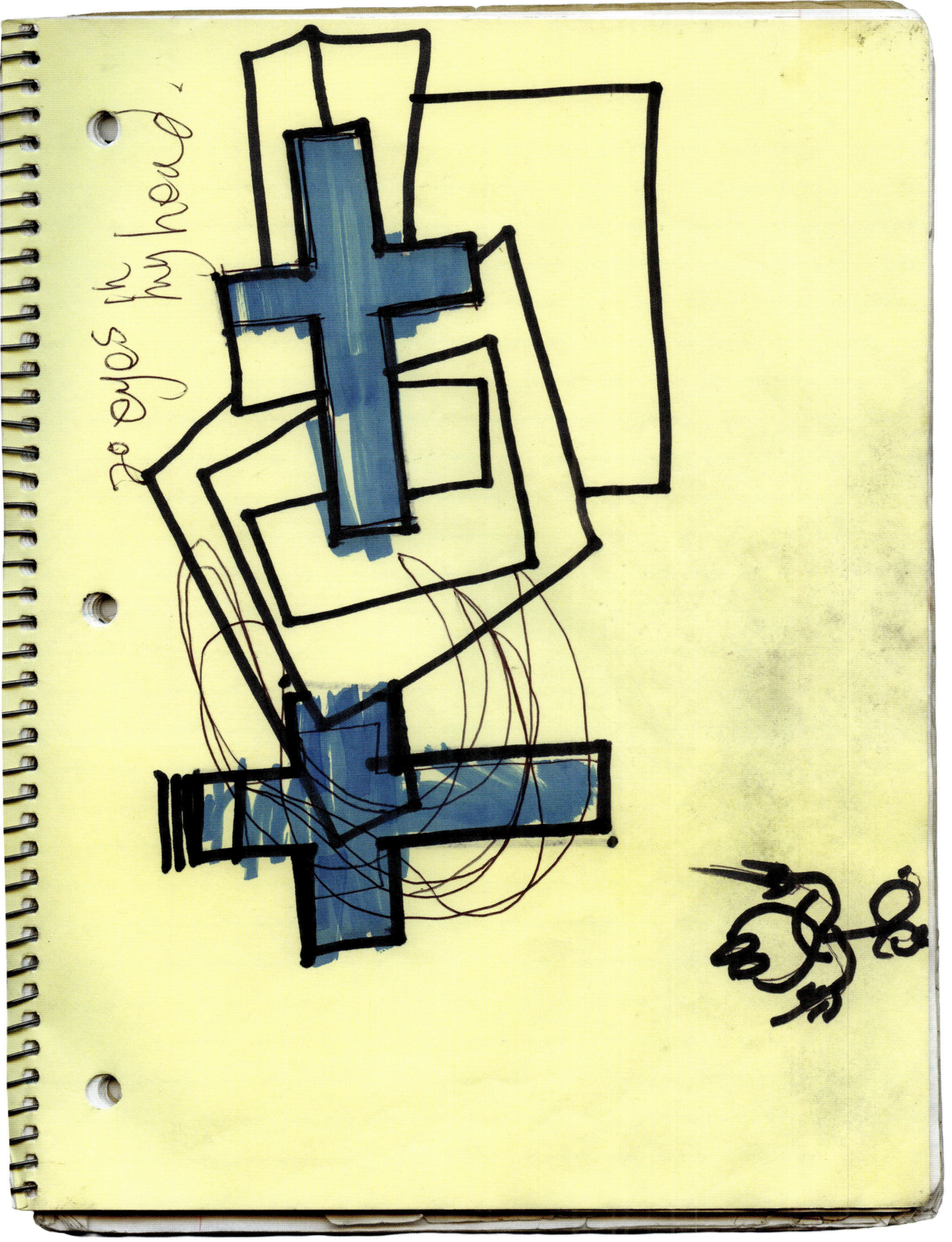

growing old

- you start stink more
- you cant take care of yourself
im old i too kare of them.
mid twentysies

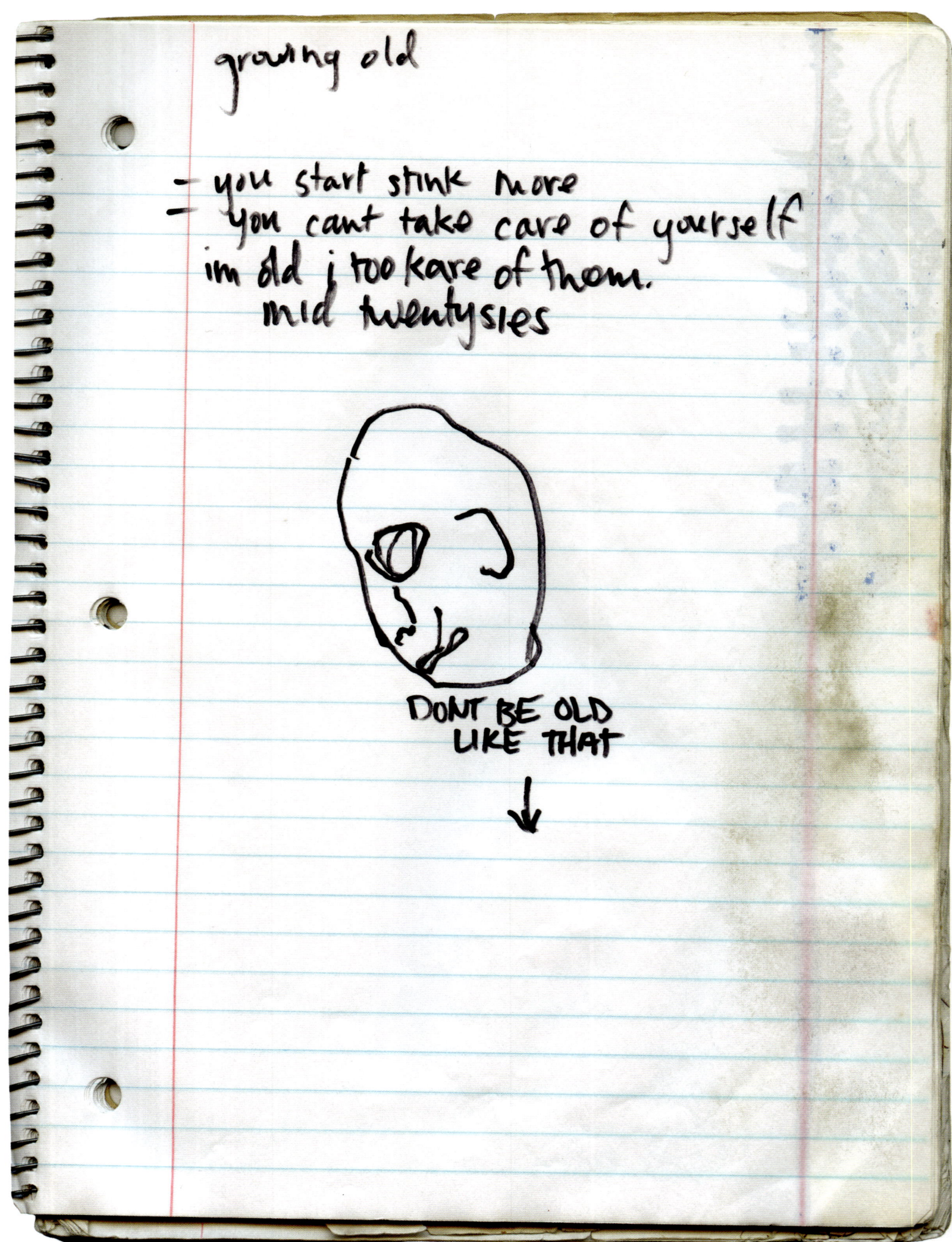

DONT BE OLD
LIKE THAT

I think that just blowing up as a band, we'd never been exposed to so much fervor, fever, so it was a weird place for us to be in. I had no intention of being a gigantic rock band. All my favorite bands are pretty small, so this daunting kind of unreality of where we were at and how it all happened so quickly made for a really fun, confusing and scary time. John Feldman was brand new at recording and his energy is fierce. He's one of the hardest working men in rock and roll music, and he just has this vibe that's just like 20 coffees in. It's pretty amazing. So the pressure from our producer at the time was really helpful. Usually I've kind of pushed away from any type of authority figure, but the way he likes to work, it really pushes me to work harder and pushes me to write better lyrics and kind of go back and rethink things.

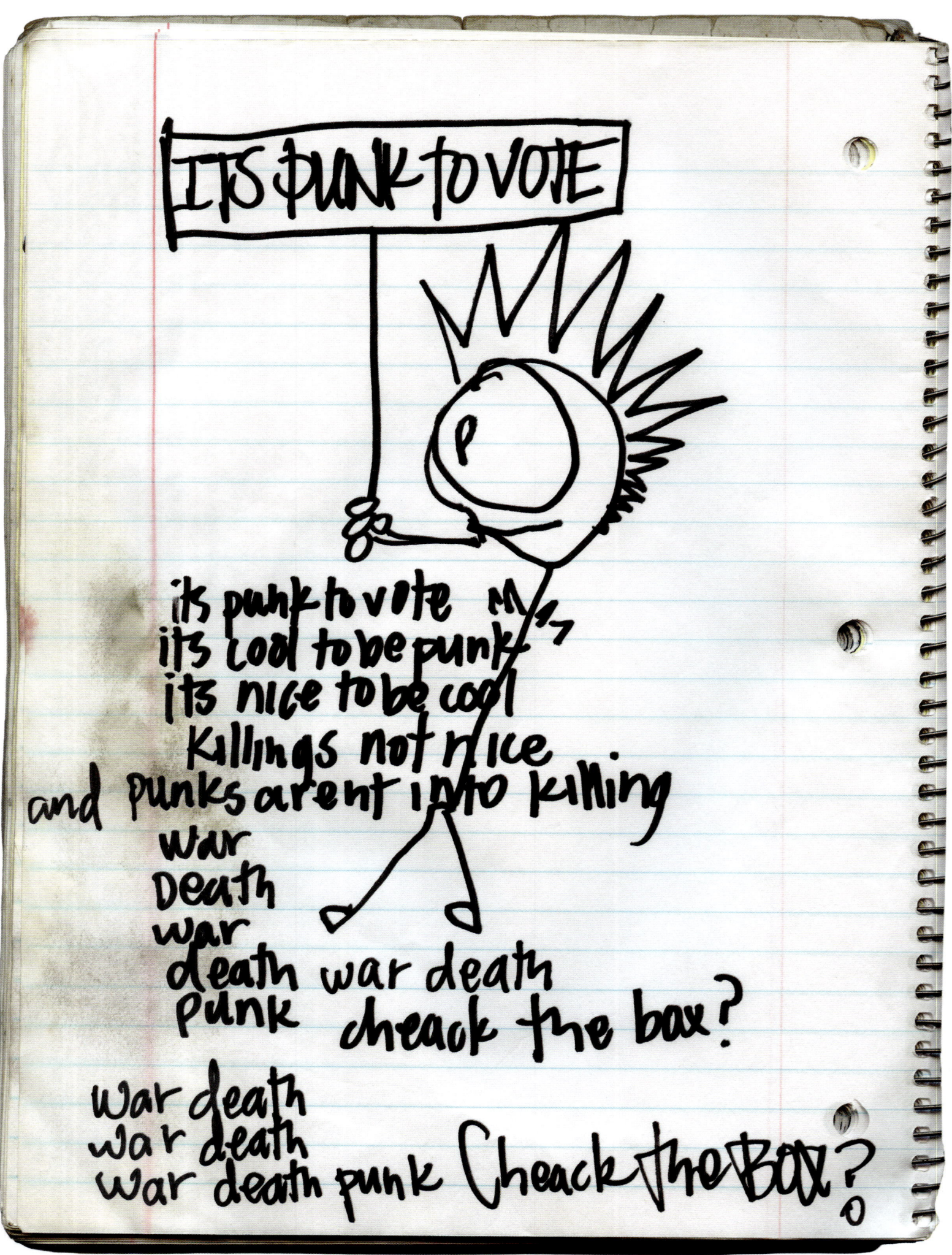

ITS PUNK TO VOTE

its punk to vote my,
its cool to be punk
its nice to be cool
    killings not nice
and punks arent into killing
    war
    death
    war
    death war death
    punk cheack the box?

war death
war death
war death punk Cheack the Box?

132

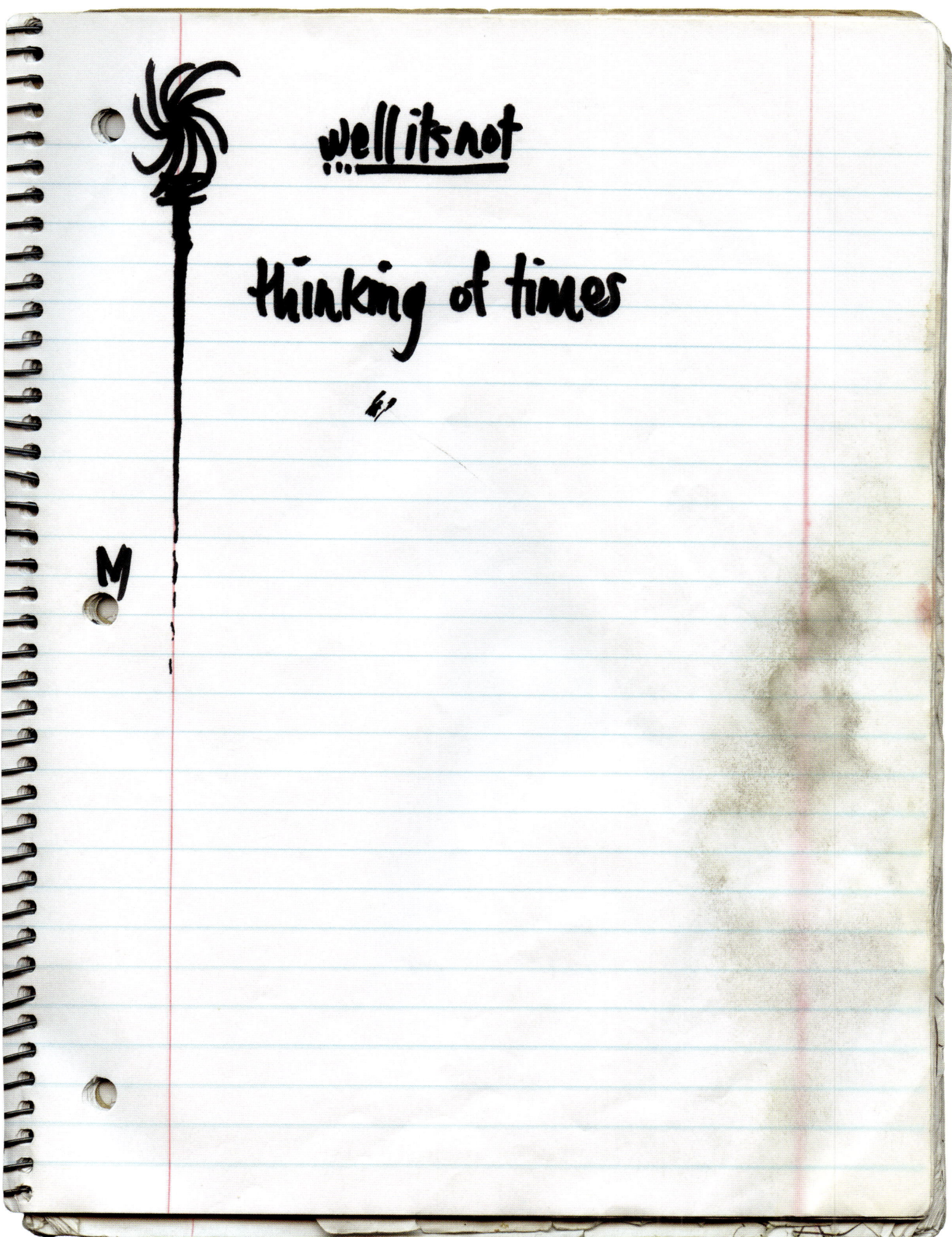

well it's not

thinking of times

i Am the leader of a revolution →
← the head of the pimple
infection . a mountain →
← with all emphasis lost
and powers my obsession →
← with power a delusion
← and i know she's naked in →
my bed now. →
← the thoughts in my head
could cut down buildings →
← But I would Rather
sing a song →
← id much rather sing a song
really rather →
← sing a song
and cut this Hate down →

← 009 009 009 009
009 009 009 009
←BIEVIOSTER
BERTO hotmail.co

i cant care now to worry im feeling
so lonely   just breaking apart
all this love in my heart.
all those feelings those yesterdays feelings
will all be lost in time
but today i've wasted away
for today is on my mind

close my eyes and
move to the back of my mind
where worries are washed
to sea   see the changes peoples
faces blurred out like sun spots
or rain drops now

i cant care to worry
im feeling so lonely

holding tight and try not to hide
i left the only worries
i had in my my hands.
a way from the light in
my eyes.
holding tight and try
not to hide
how i feel and knowing
means nothing now

There was a lot of that. Cool. It's all very different today. It's kind of run with it. We recorded a song a day and just throw it at the wall and see what sticks. It seemed like back then it was a real process for each song. Each song had its own life and not, they don't have that today, but it was just a more focused and more serious amount of time spent on each song. I mean, recording the record took us about a year, I think. And that's unrealistic for records nowadays. You work on a record for two or three weeks and pop. Not much time for development.

sure break a sweat
you've done it again
  because they told you not to
because you'll wear your heart out

I cant focus
   or halfway see
and spitting true ink
  out onto the page
    is taking so much energy
these hangovers are so reminding
   of the way i love to hate to be

ive searched the side streets
to try to find me
secrets known
could i have possibley
lost what i hover
had at all
balled up
depths
on

i walked this lonely all a lonely
searching mostly sticky ~~visually~~
visual
deeper the energy

a wise man once told me
to hold my tung as he swallowed
his could i

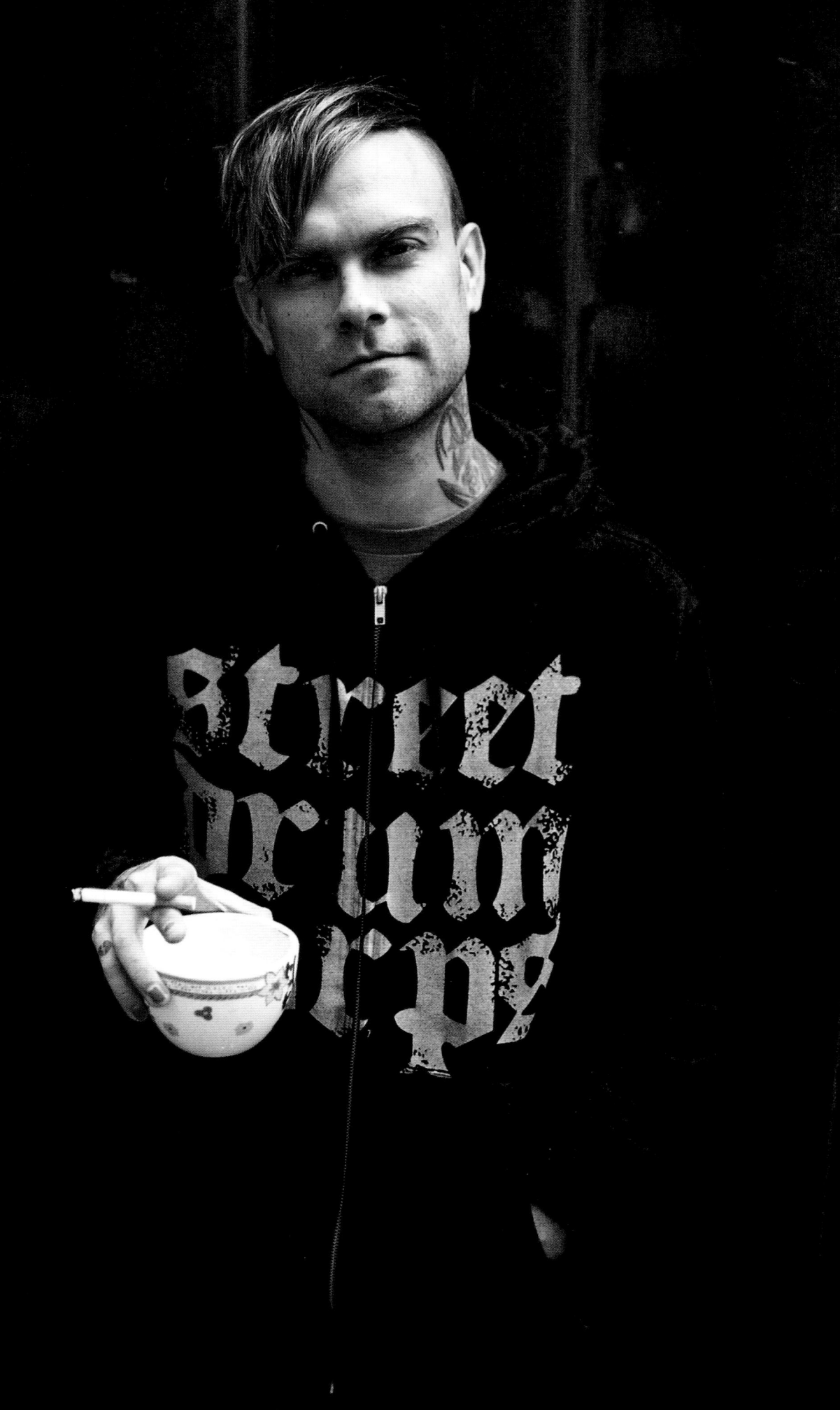

its not me

buried ~~butanethehtothe~~ wreakage
my soul

its not me

its not me

free from the torment of sin
all this im giving up
much as the sun must decide to give in
explode into orange and hear all the
voices sing praises with hymns
~~the birth of the night sky~~
marks the birth of a change
im free from the torment of sin (within)
all this im giving up

its not me

over and over again
a light with a sharpened edge
cuts through the black empty space we call sky
beginning the cycle that stays
and i know in my heart we all die
like the day and the night
like the sun in the sky
        all this im giving up.

is there another side
beyond the black & white
a place i could meet you by
a place on the other side
i'll let you know when i go
i'll let you know when i'm gone

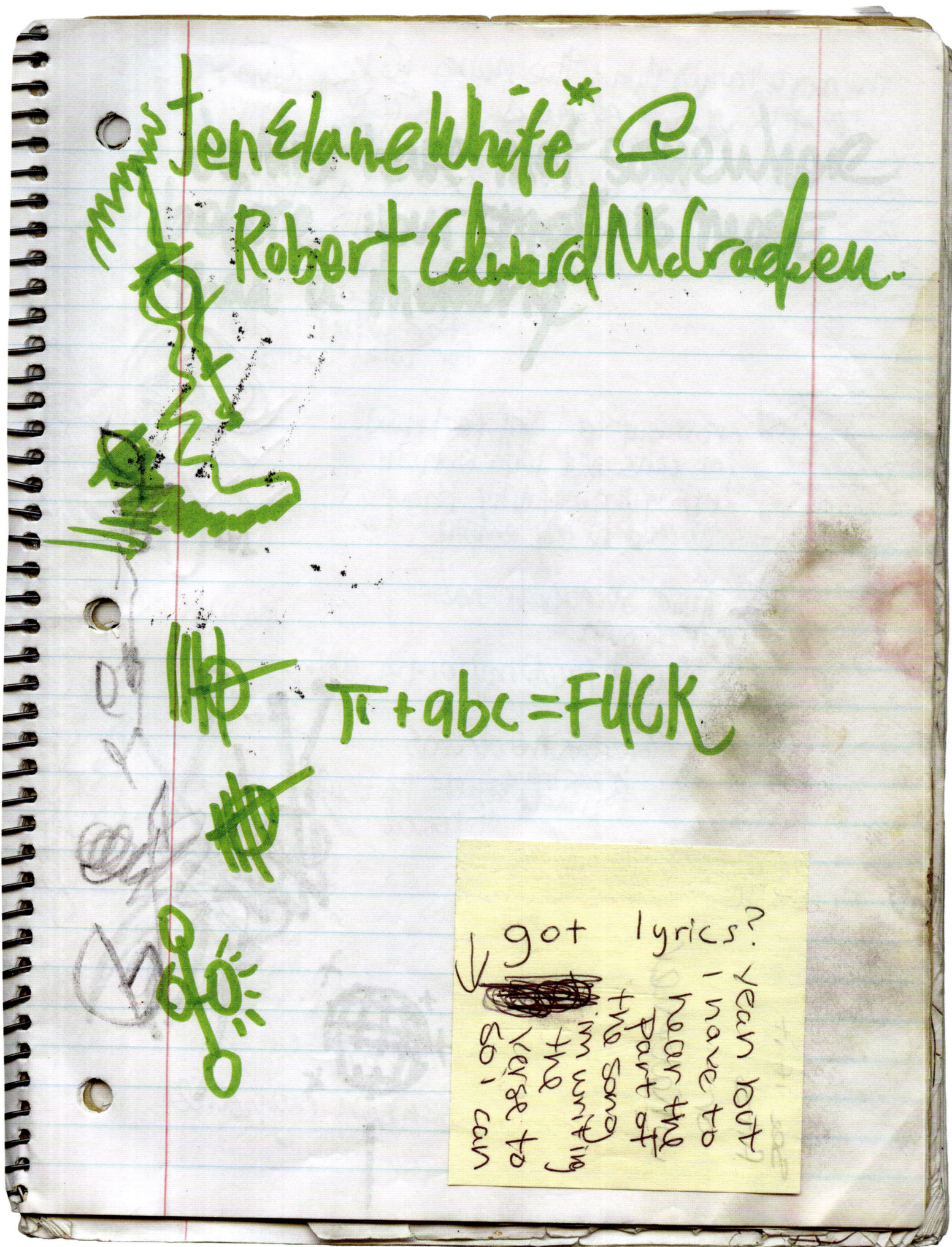

Jen Elane White*

Robert Edward McCracken.

$\pi + abc = FUCK$

got lyrics? yeah (out)
I have to hear the
part of the song
(I'm writing
the verse to
so I can

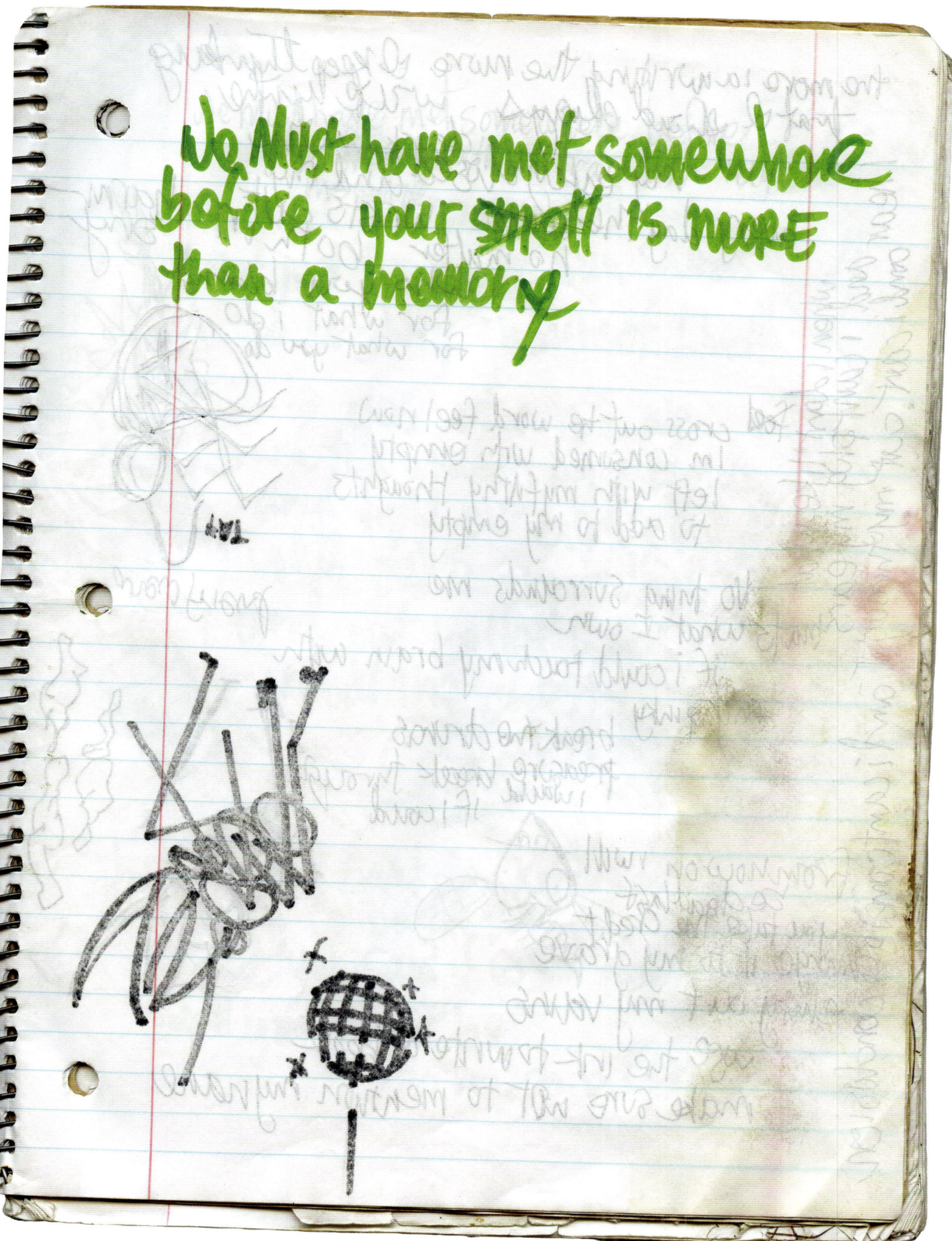

We must have met somewhere
before your smell is more
than a memory

the more i a writing the more i keep thinking
that i should always write in the
dark with
my eyes closed and my
every day the same wrists cut in harm—
no matter both in ony
who you blame
for what i do
for what you do

feel cross out the word feel now
I'm consumed with empty
left with my filthy thoughts
to add to my empty

No thing surrounds me
thats what I own
if i could touch my brain with
my pinky

break the drums
preasure i would break through
if i could

from now on i will
be dead last
you take the credit
charge it to my grave
empty out my veins
use the ink to write
make sure not to mention my name

when i don't like what
i hear and i can't plug my ears
and i can't cut my thought and i can't come to conclusion

FAT

new friend

I still have a lot of journals from the last four records. I think some of my best poetry and best lyrics, I'm constantly going back and stealing from my own work. It's part of the process for me to kind of get everything in one place. Like I said, a lot of the records nowadays are just written on the phone and bouncing lyrics back and forth. We have a process with writing nowadays that everybody sits in one room and everybody gives ideas for everything. So the whole band will be giving lyrical ideas and whole band giving drum ideas and creates a different vibe, lyrics maybe I would've never thought of before. So back in the day I wrote 'em all by myself and now everybody helps out with everything.

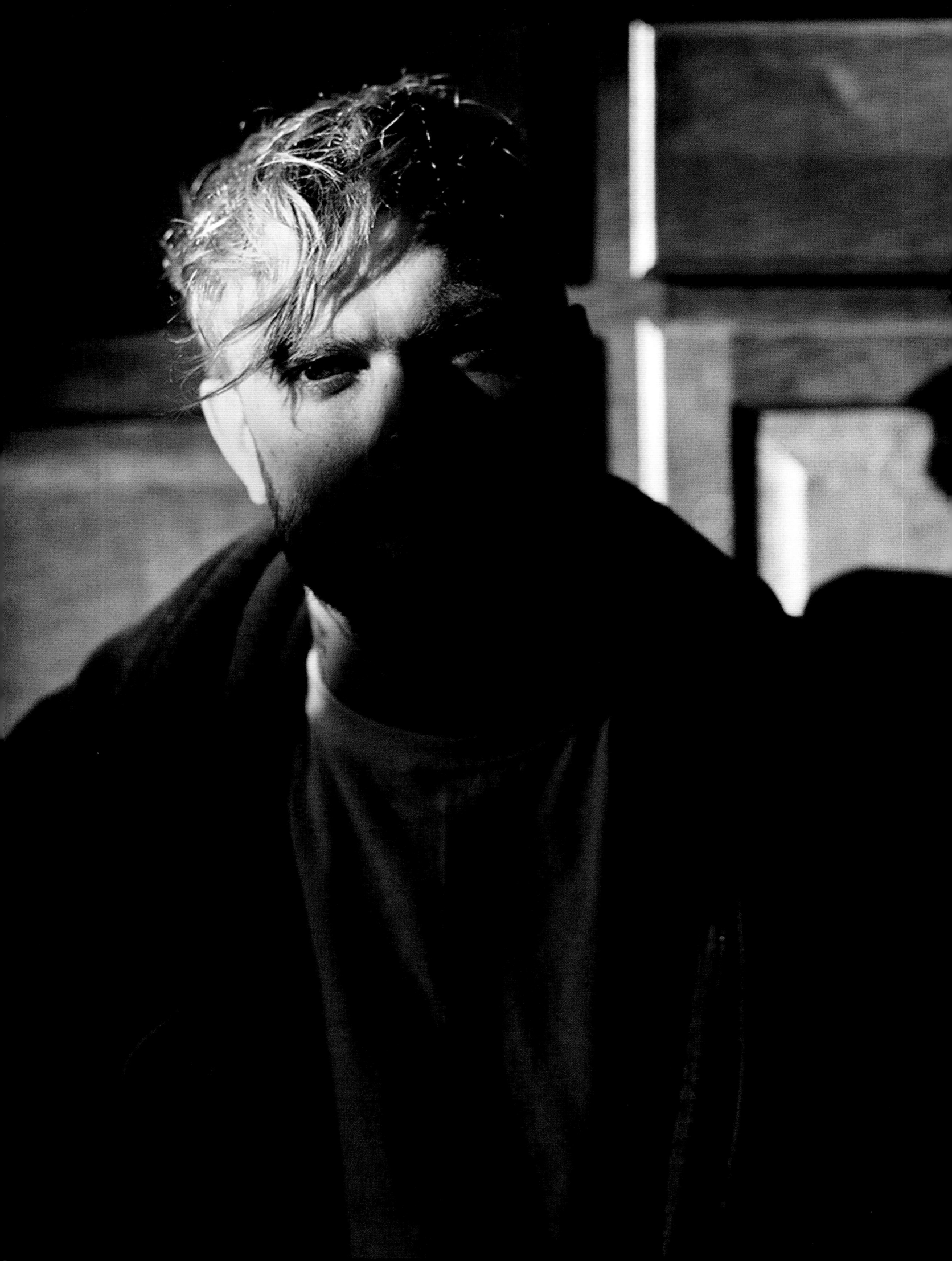

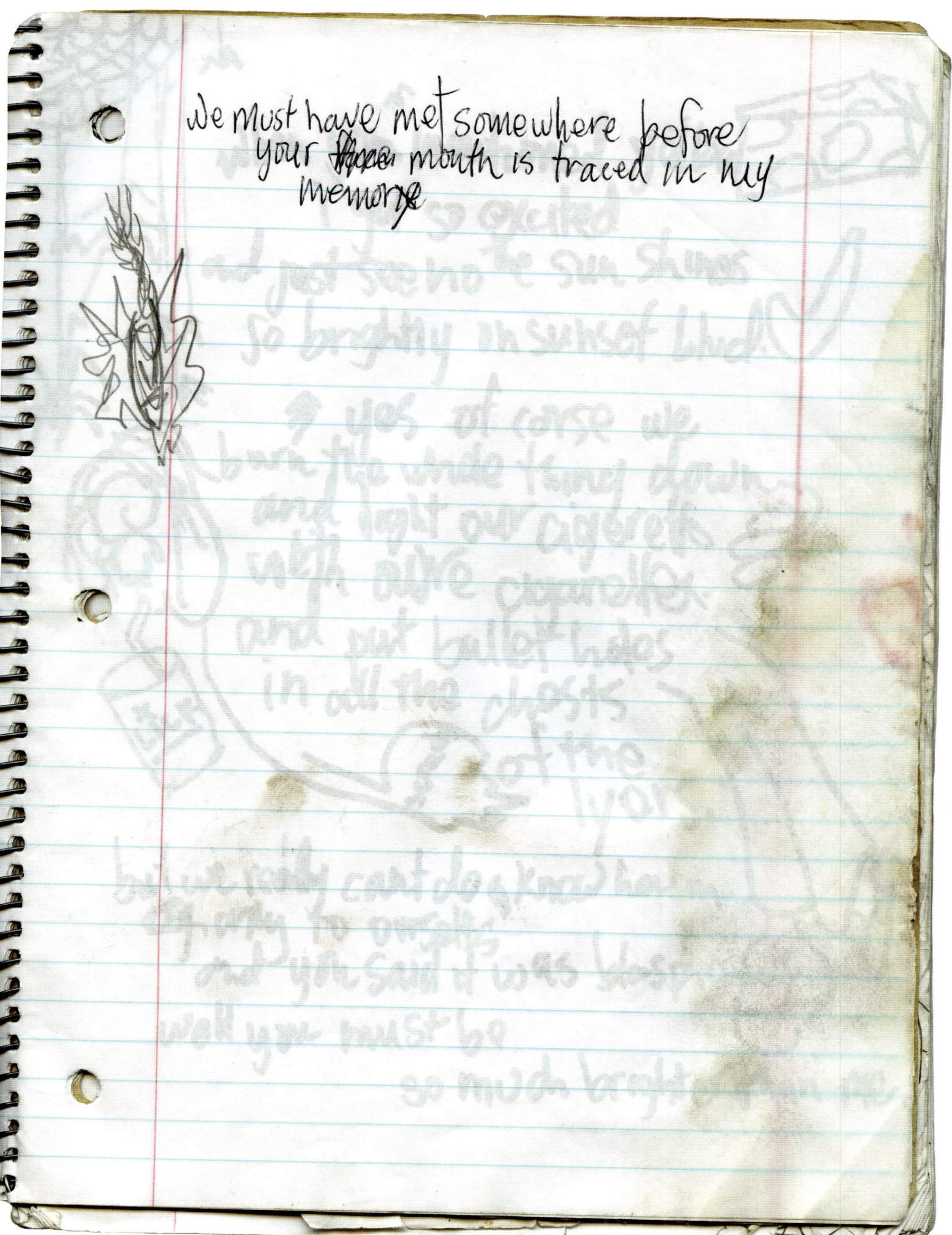

We must have met somewhere before
your ~~three~~ mouth is traced in my
memory

when you mentioned yellow
i got so excited
and just see no the sun shines
so brightly in sunset blvd.

yes of corse we
burn the whole thing down
and light our cigeretts
with oure ciparettes.
and put bullet holes
in all the chests
of the
lyors.

but we really cant do a know harm
only to ourselfs
and you said it was blasphomy
well you must be
so much brighter than me

in your eyes / with that face
i cracked a smile and let go of
everything. all at once ~~but~~ like the first
time ~~whatever time~~ I caught fire
              that
         lay with me stay right here
    stay and lets sleep till the sun
         burns out

   you can stay and watch me fall
   and of coarse ill ask for help
   we could take our heads off
stay in bed. ~~just make love thats~~
         ~~and~~
      and just make love all thats
              all

RIP
PORSHA
& BRET

149

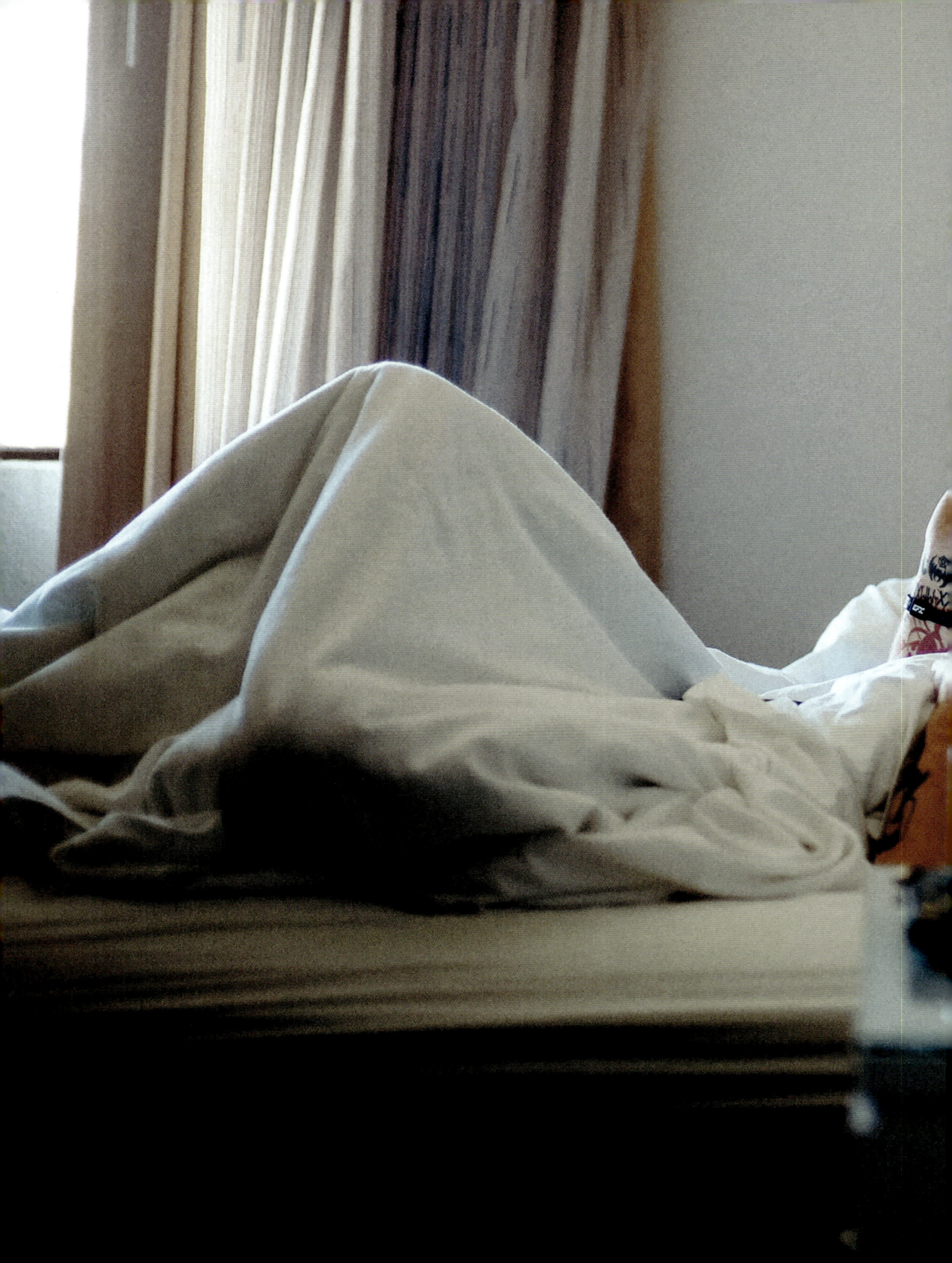

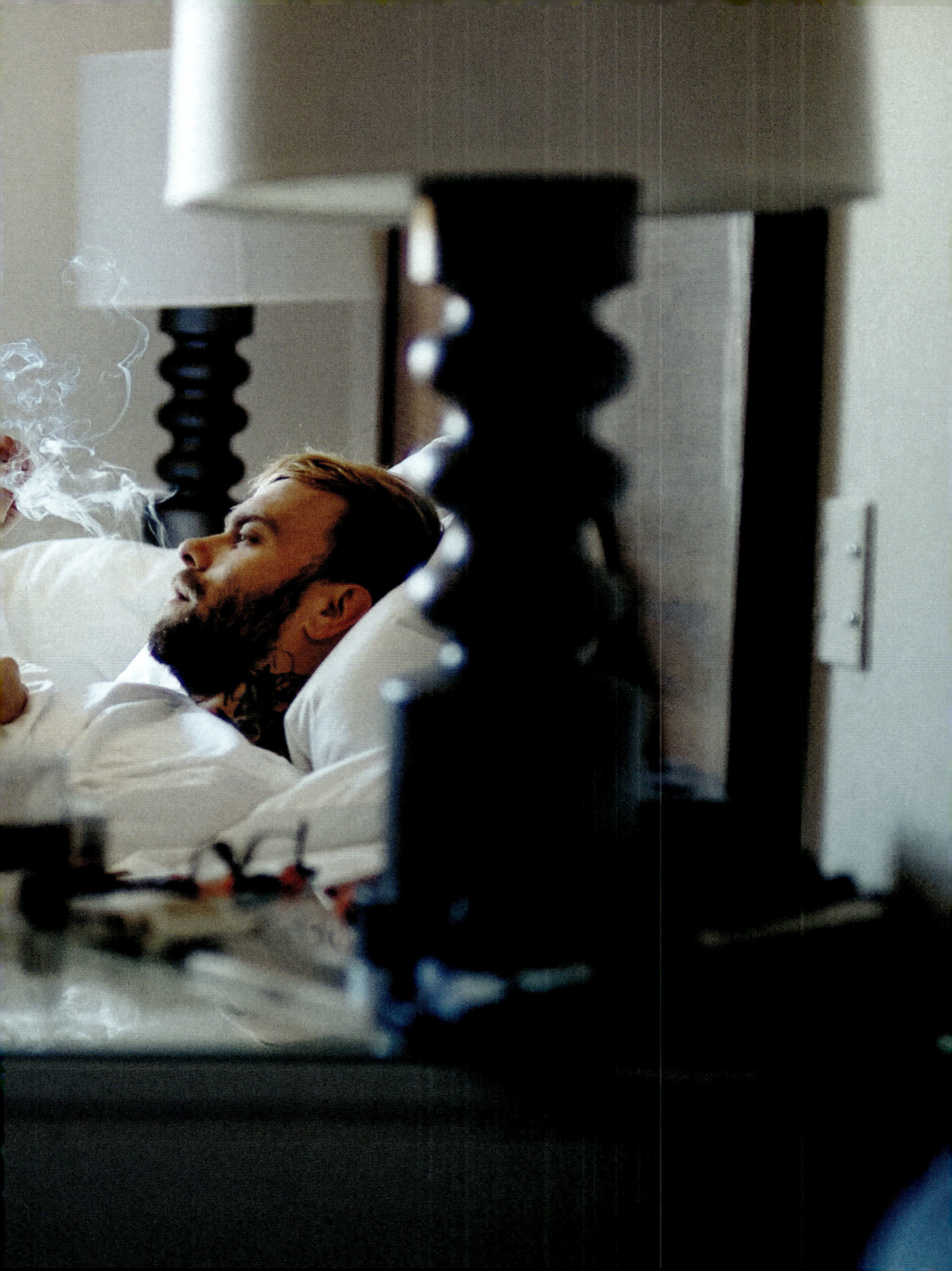

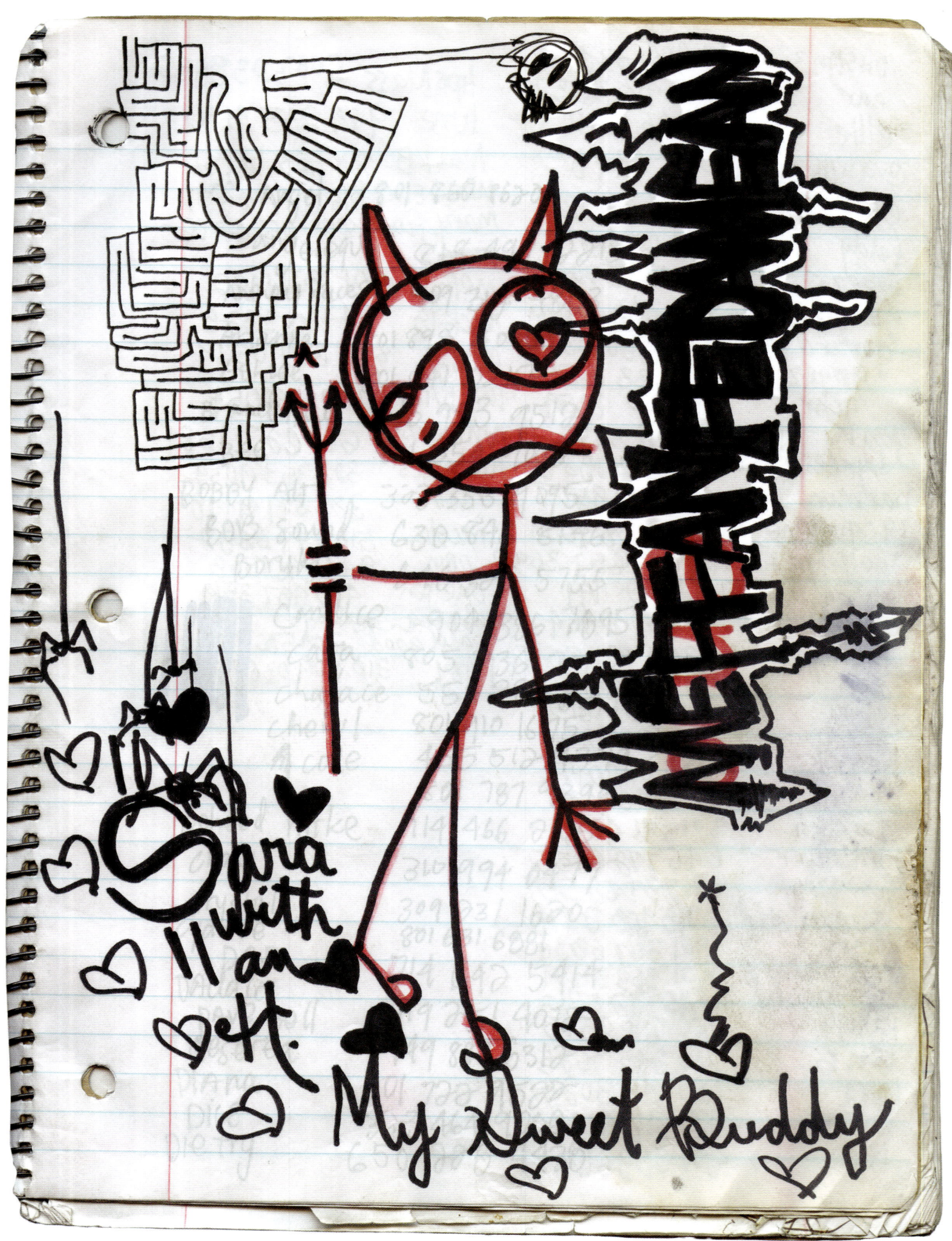

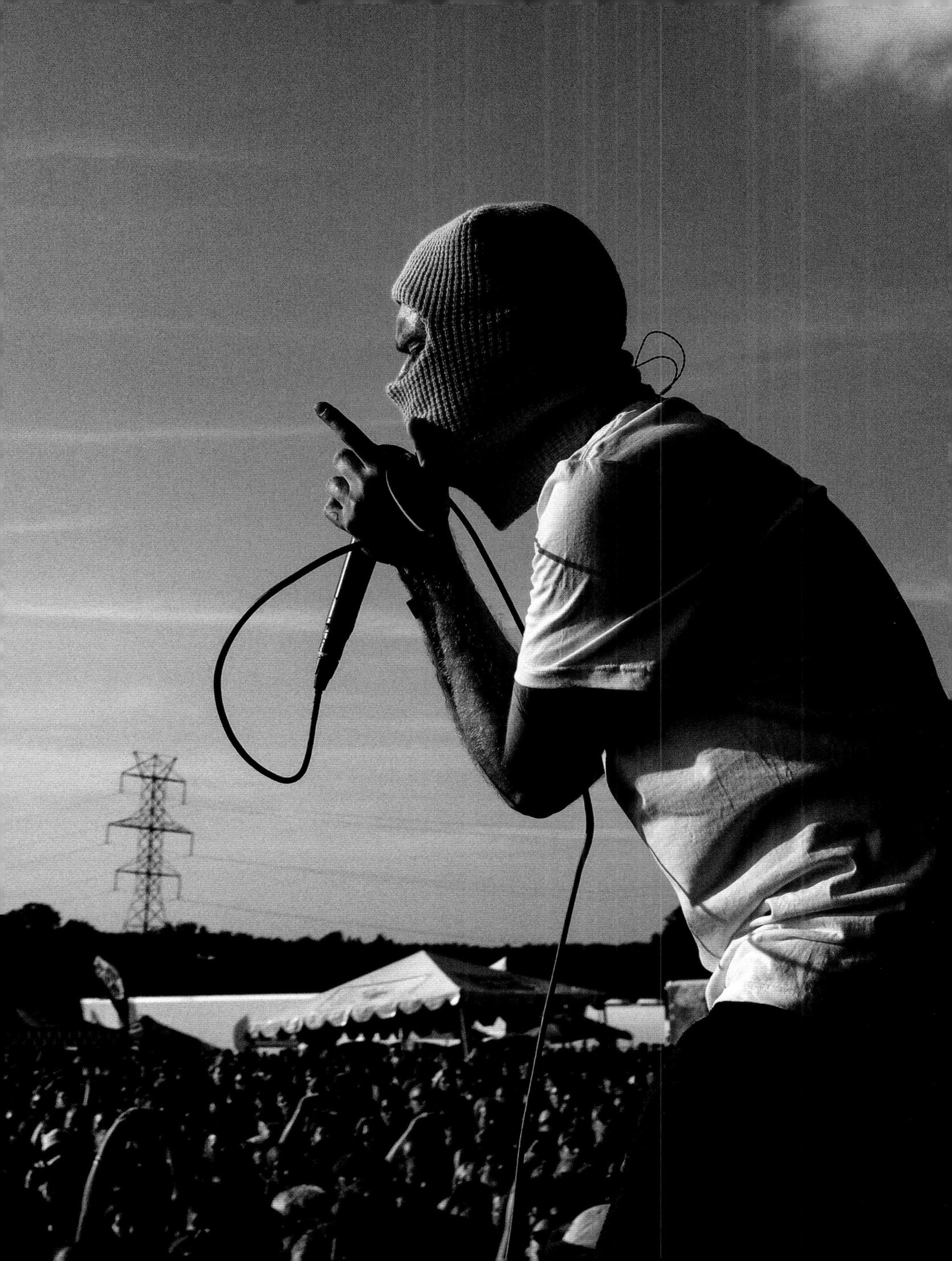

I've always been really good with lyrics. I've always been really good with poetry and sitting down to write something out. I always feel like I succeed to a certain degree. Definitely having a stockpile of old work to reflect on helps a lot. But yeah, no, I've never really felt like I'm in the weeds with any lyrics or that I can't get it out of me. I find that when I write exactly how I feel, it can relate. Everybody can relate to tragedy or loss or those kinds of things. Confident in the moment and then really hard and scary to put out because I know how the world is nowadays and how the internet is. I just try not to look. But yeah, it's a bit daunting and scary once it's time to put it out. But I always feel like I succeeded in the process.

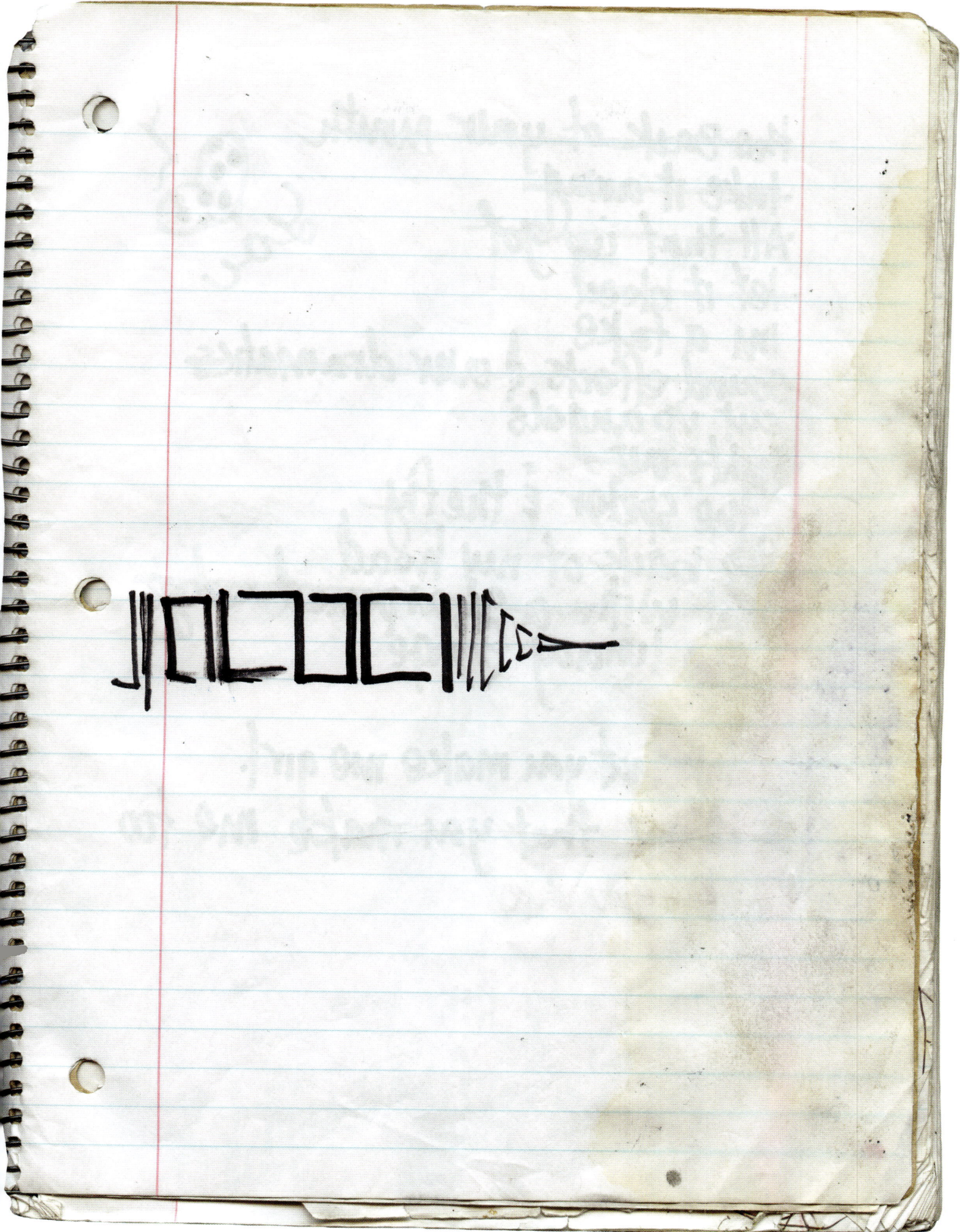

the Back of your mouth
take it away
All that iv got
let it bleed
im a take
sound effects & over dramatics
cut up angels
lights out
the spider & the fly
the back of my head
tight with a sharpened edge
the lunacy fringe

you

I think that you make me girl.
& i think that you make me too
I think you make

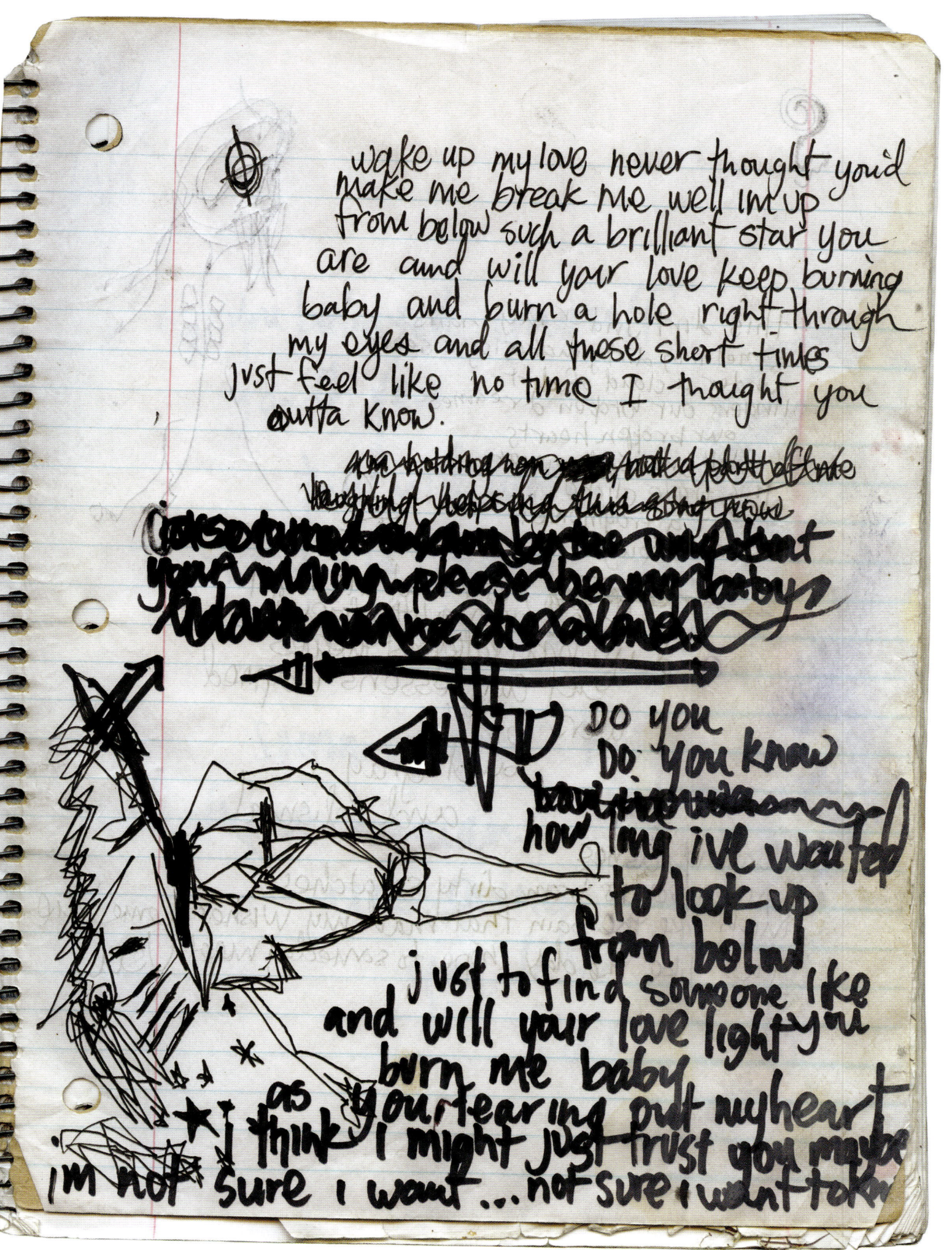

wake up my love never thought you'd
make me break me well im up
from below such a brilliant star you
are and will your love keep burning
baby and burn a hole right through
my eyes and all these short times
just feel like no time I thought you
outta know.

DO YOU
DO YOU KNOW
how long ive waited
to look up
from below
just to find someone like
and will your love light you
burn me baby
as your tearing out my heart
I think I might just trust you maybe
im not sure i want...not sure i want take

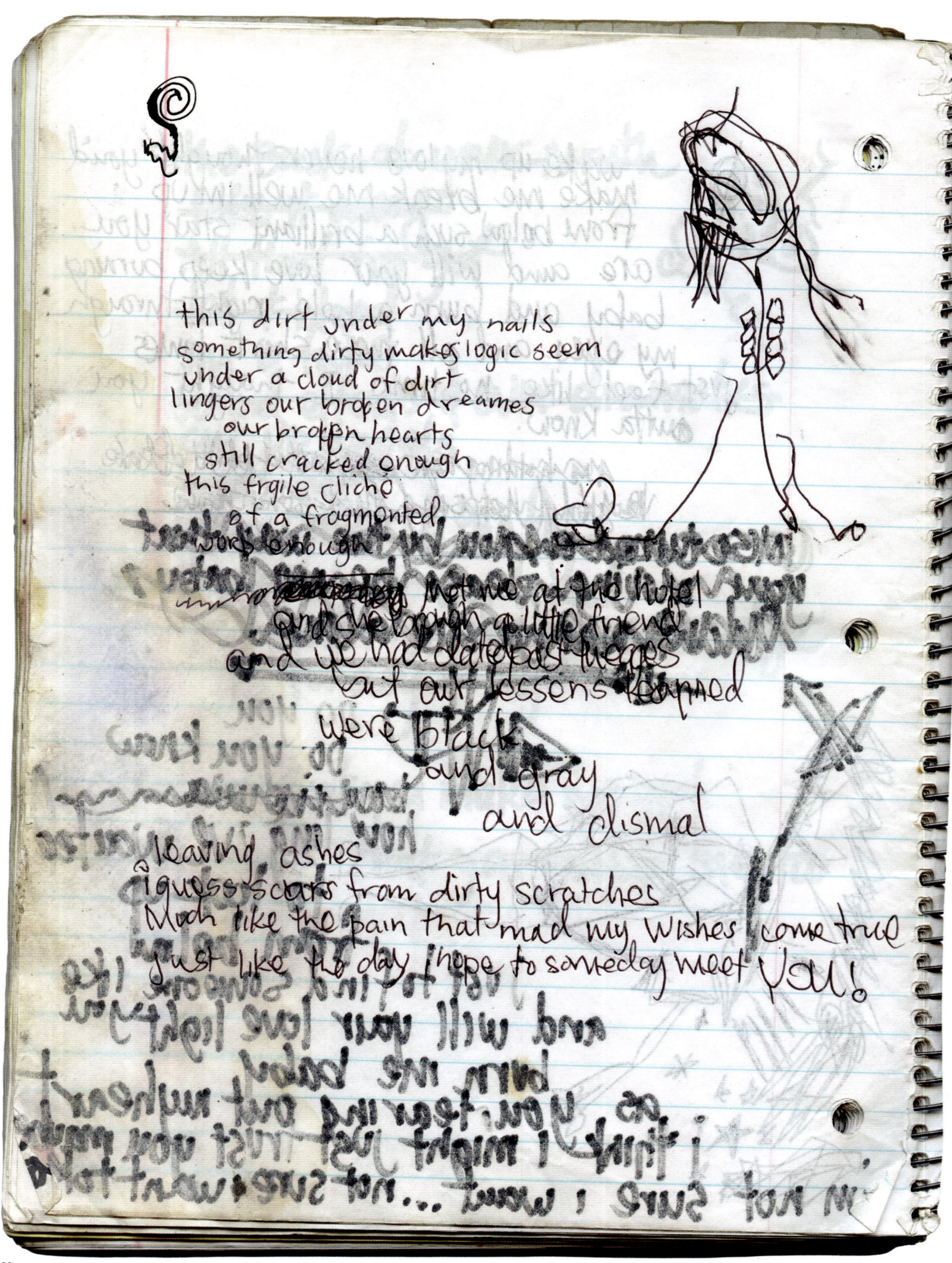

this dirt under my nails
something dirty makes logic seem
under a cloud of dirt
lingers our broken dreames
     our broken hearts
   still cracked enough
this fragile cliche
   of a fragmented
 world enough

~~met me at the hotel~~
~~and she brough a little friend~~
~~and we had date bar themes~~
~~out our lessons learned~~
  were black
       and gray
            and dismal

 leaving ashes
i guess scars from dirty scratches
Much like the pain that mad my wishes come true
just like the day I hope to someday meet YOU!

Some of my favorite lyrics. It's like if other people know the artist, then of course we get it. We can bond with it, but now don't do this anymore. Try to recite some of my favorite lyrics from artists to people who aren't familiar with that band or that group, because it always is just kind of like the fuck. Something about the connection between music and words that's so powerful. It's like smell or taste. It can transport you back exactly to that moment where you first heard it or brings up tons and tons of memories.

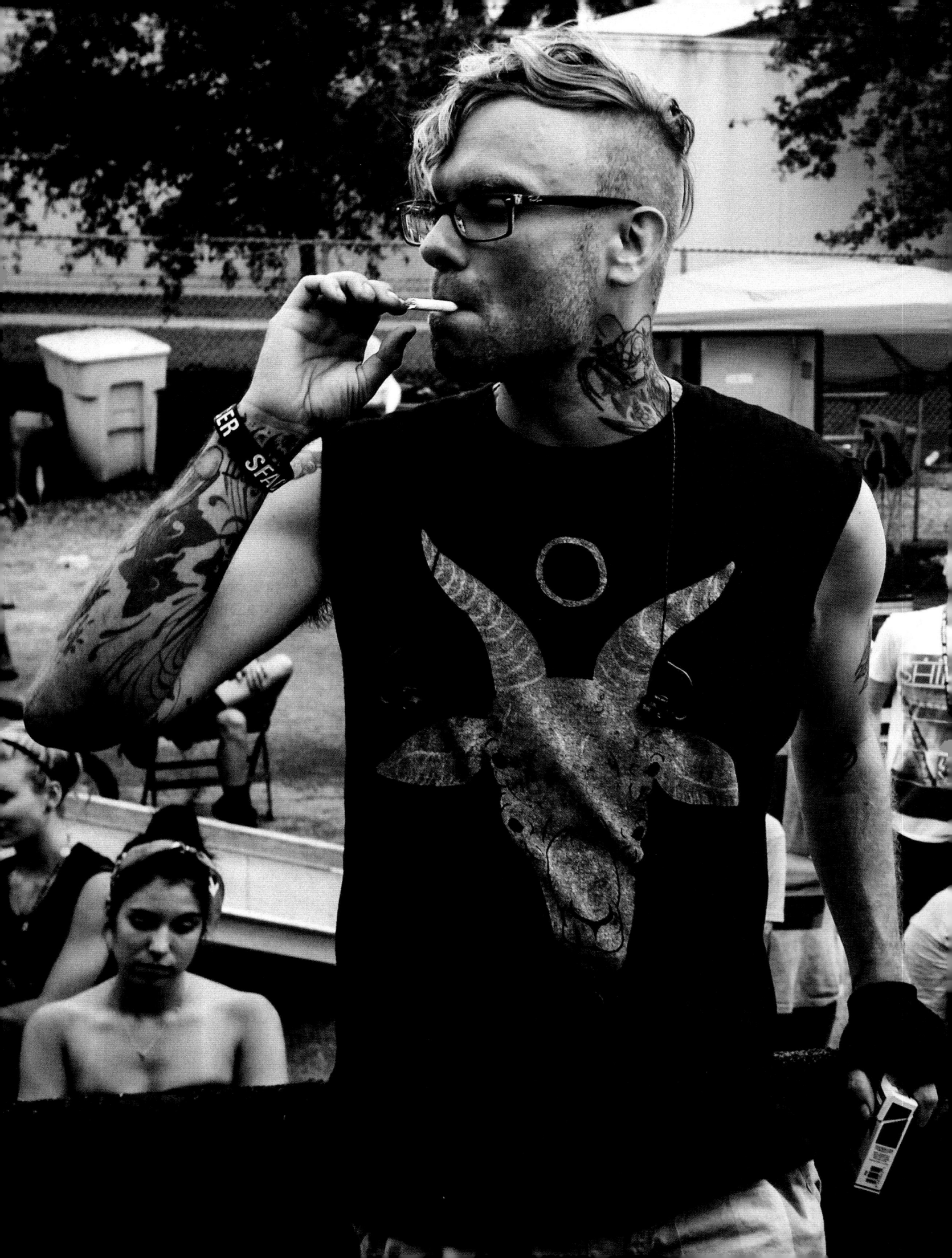

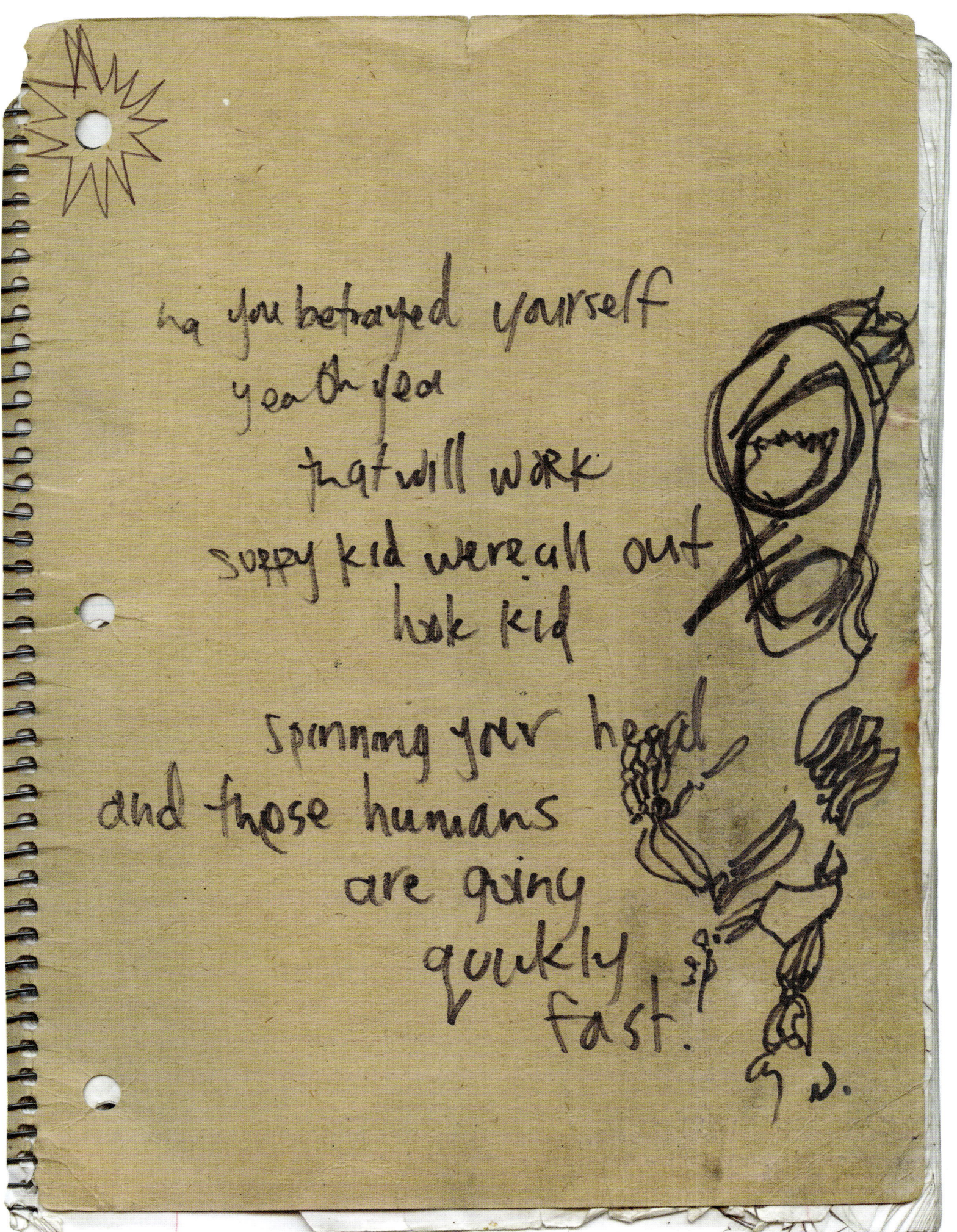

ha you betrayed yourself
yeah yea
just will work
soppy kid were all out
look kid

spinning your head
and those humans
are going
quickly
fast.

ꓱꓱꓒ

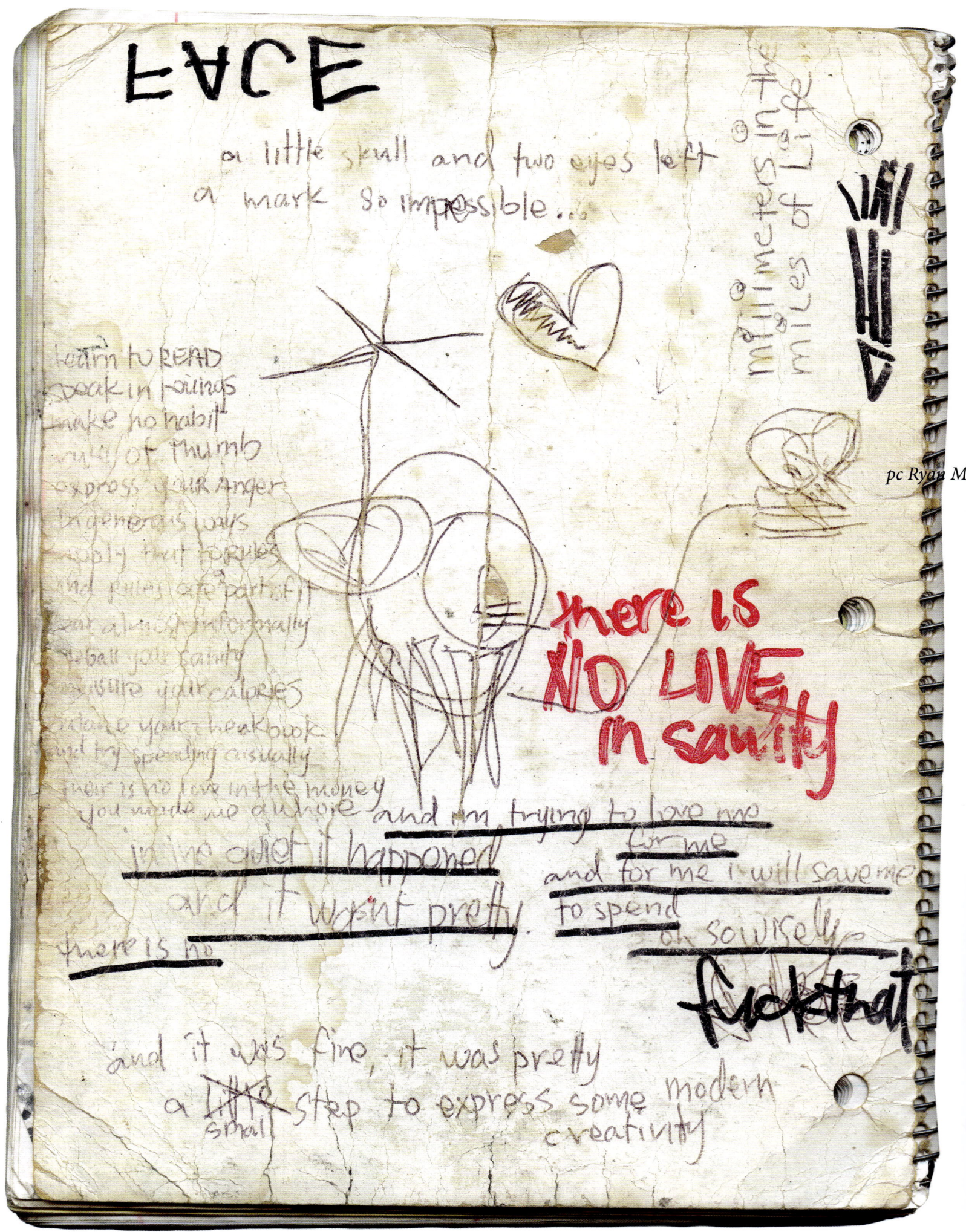

a little skull and two eyes left
a mark so impossible...

© millimeters in the
miles of Life

learn to READ
speak in pounds
make no habit
rules of thumb
express your Anger
in generous ways
apply that forRules
and rules are part of
eat a lunch informally
eyeball your sanity
measure your calories
balance your checkbook
and try spelling casually

their is no love in the money
you made me a whore and i'm trying to love me
for me
in the quiet it happened and for me i will save me
and it wasn't pretty. to spend
there is no on yourself

there is
NO LIVE
in sanity

fuckthat

and it was fine, it was pretty
a little step to express some modern
small creativity

pc Ryan M

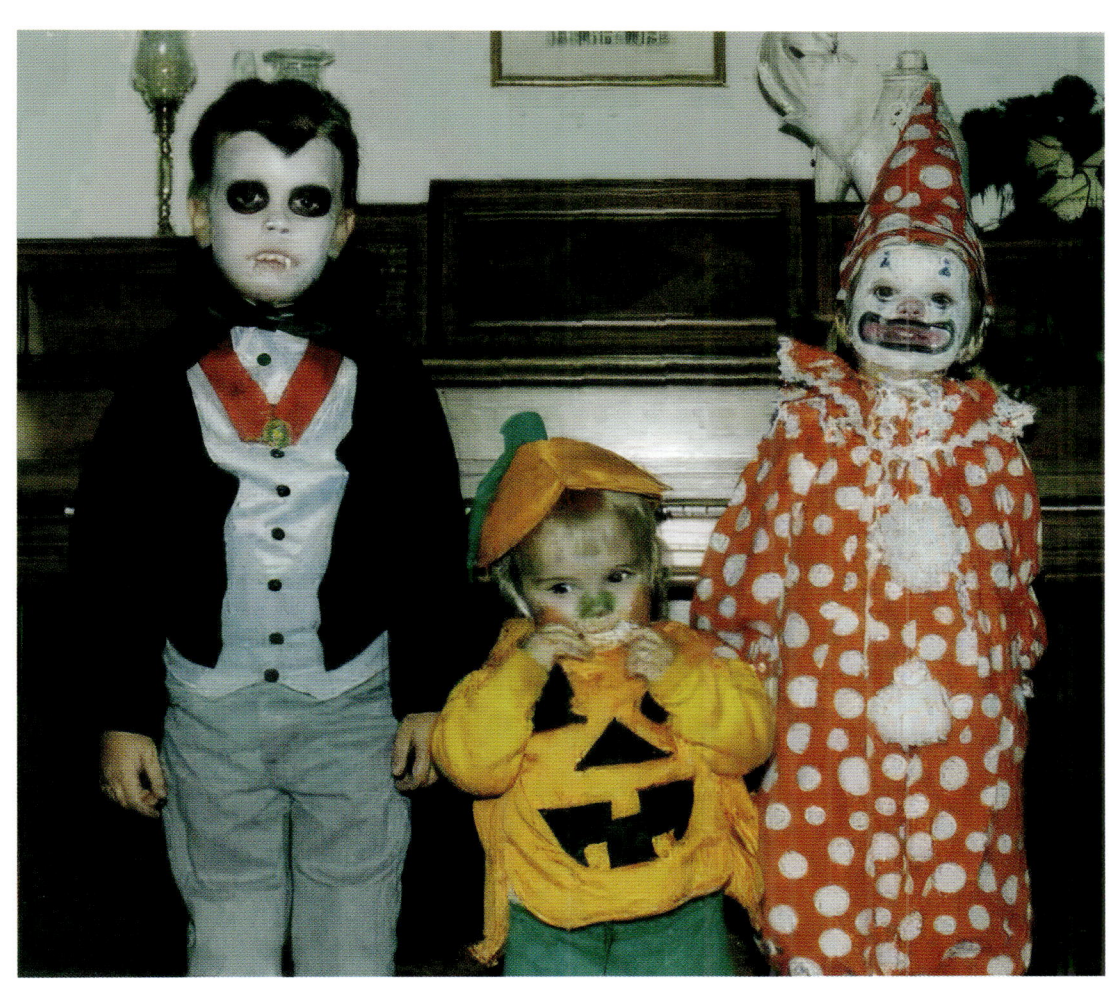

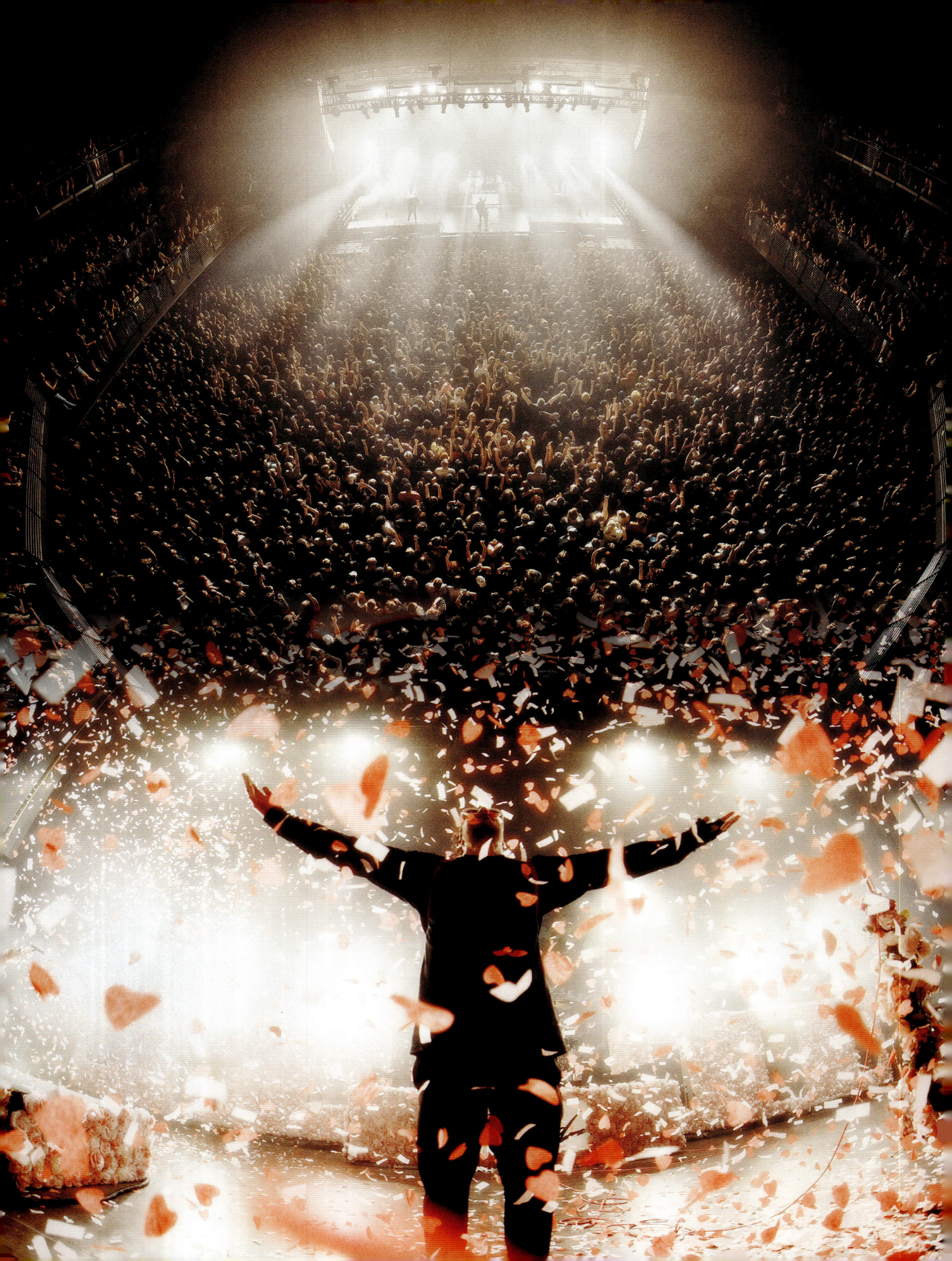

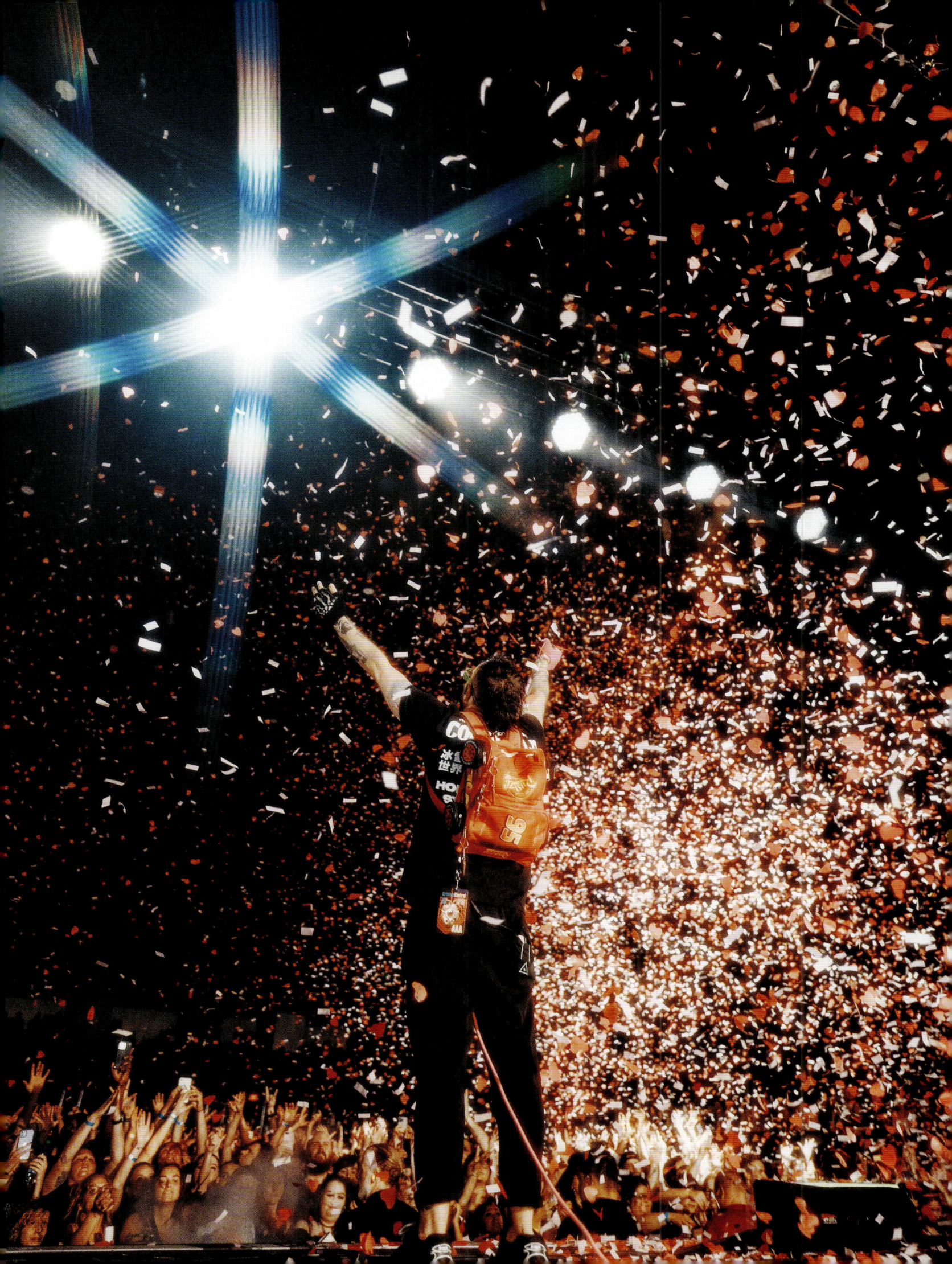

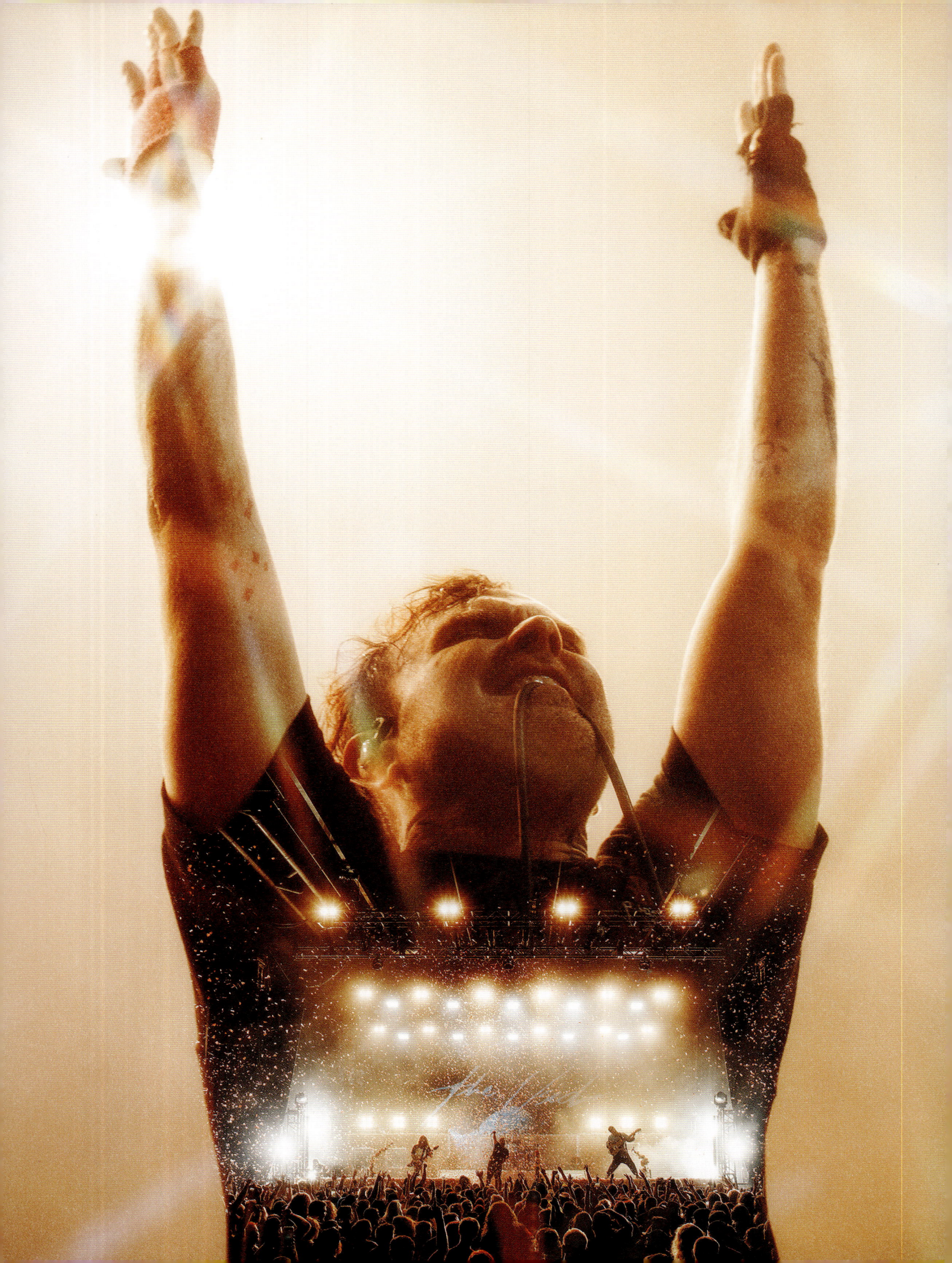

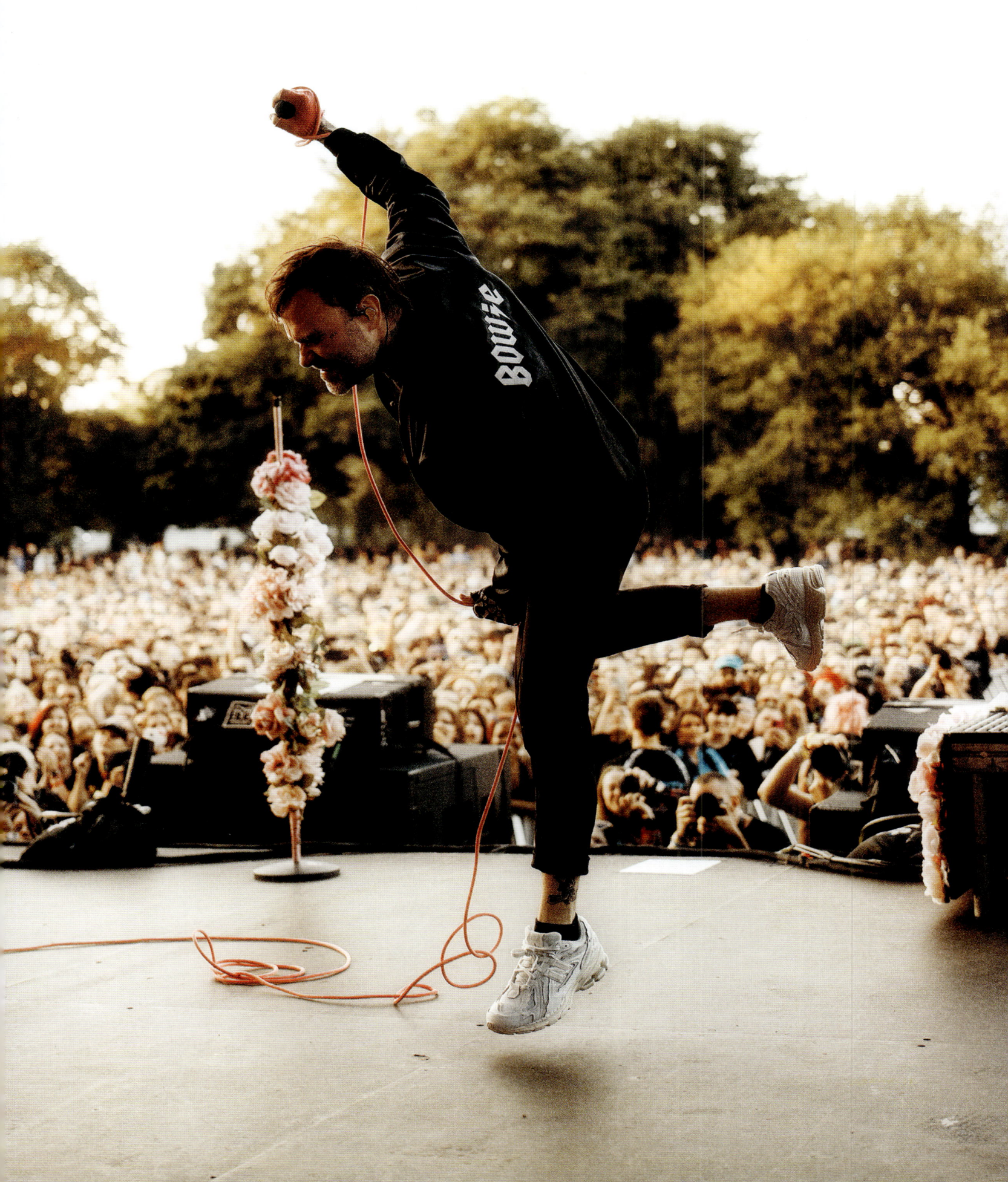

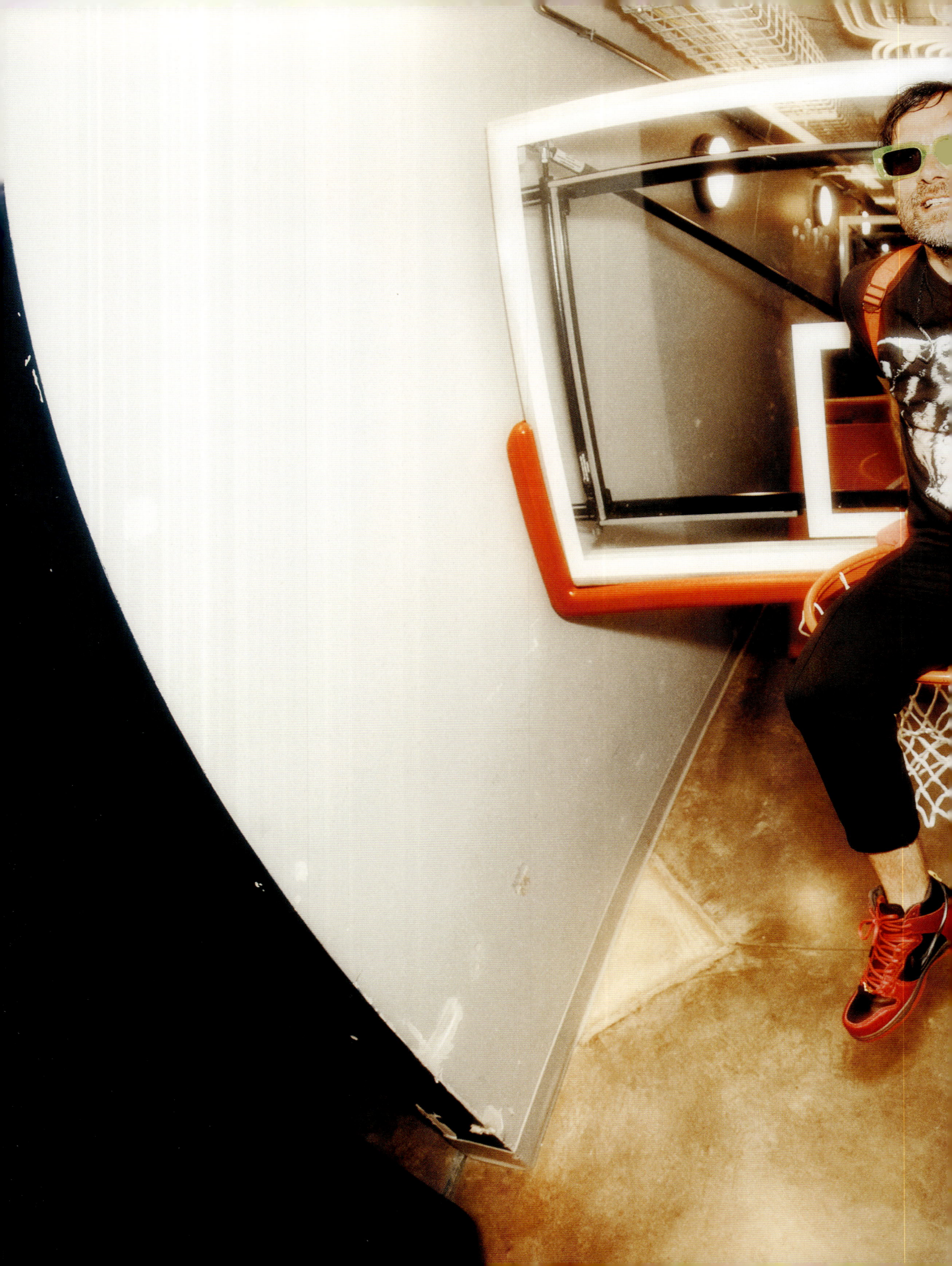

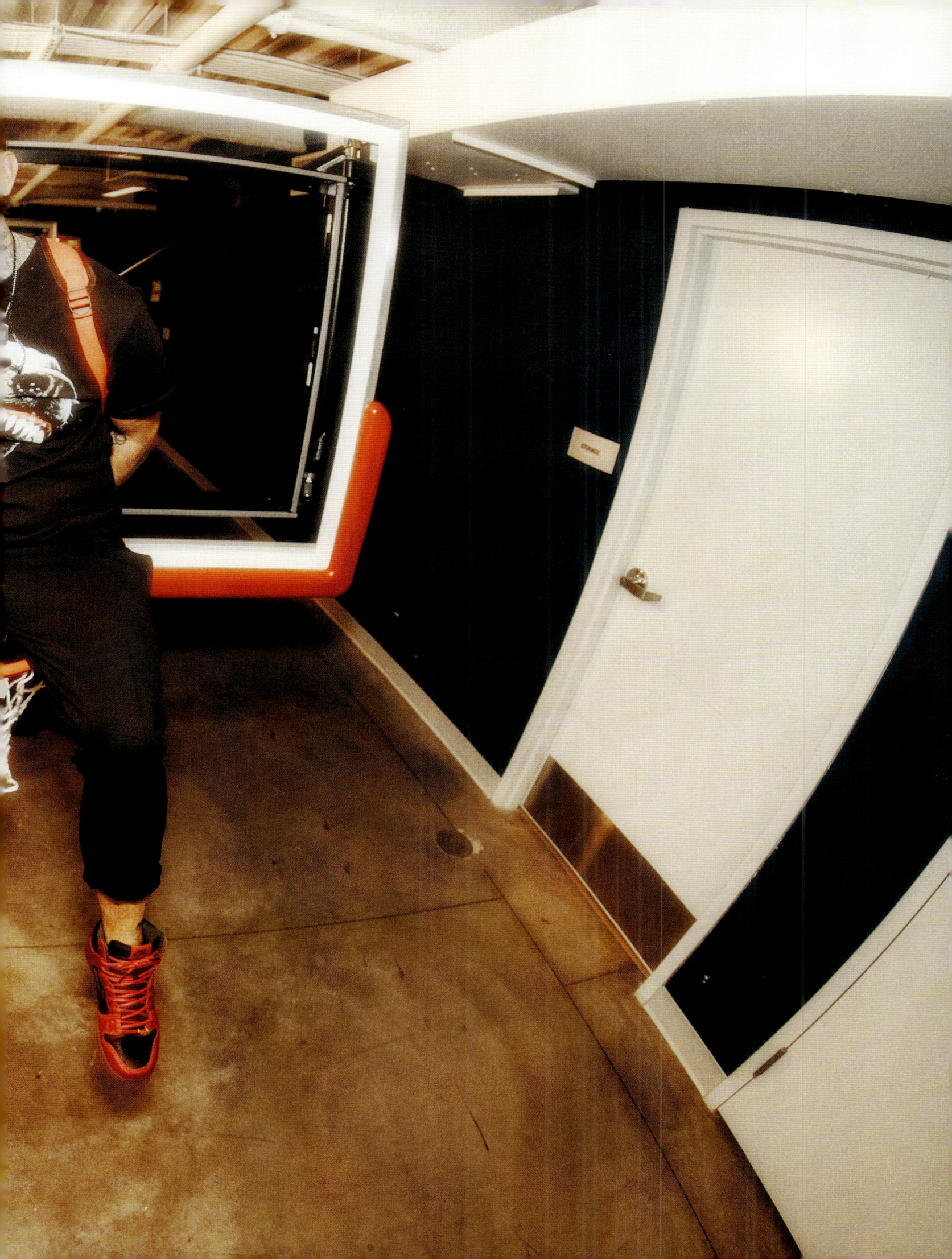

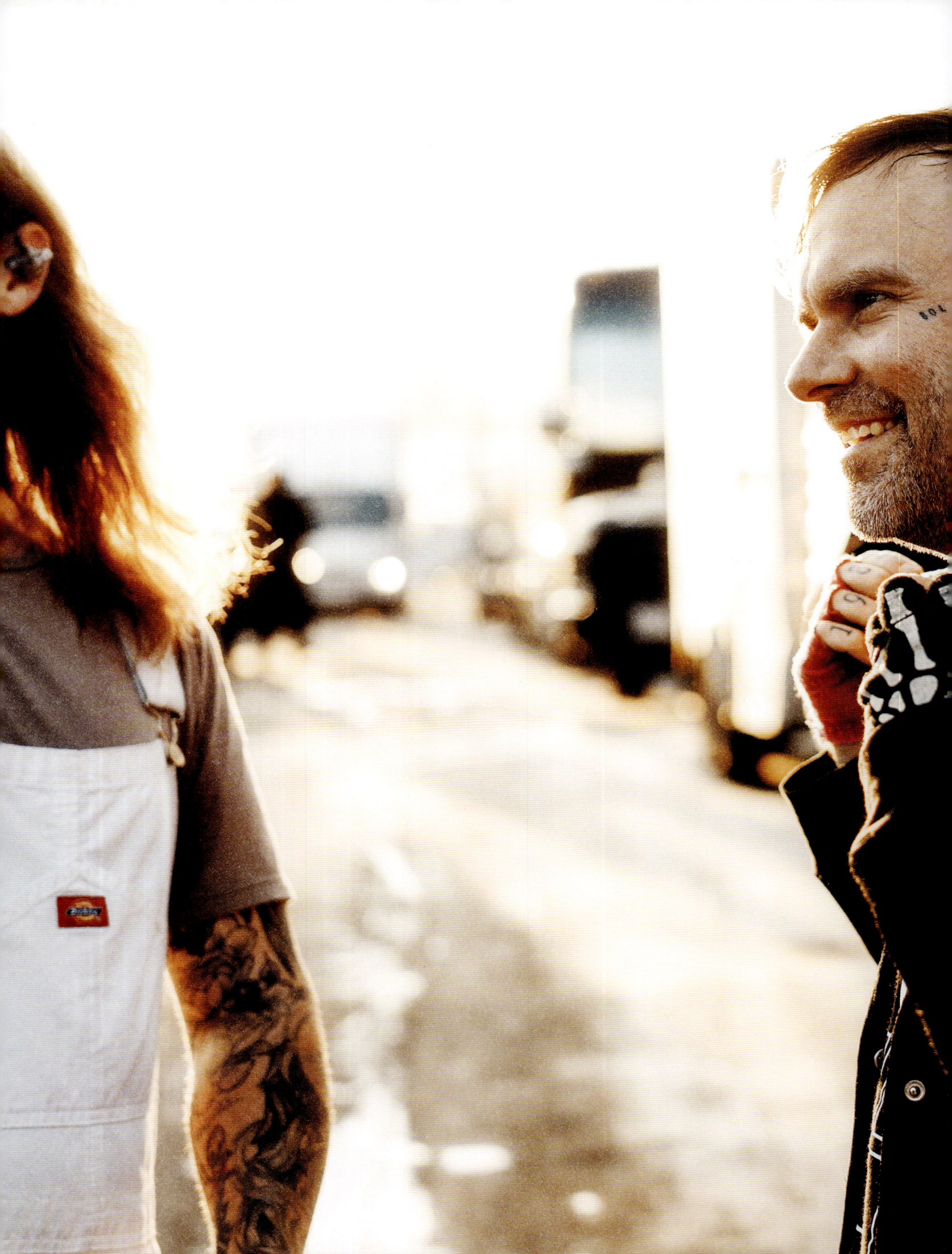

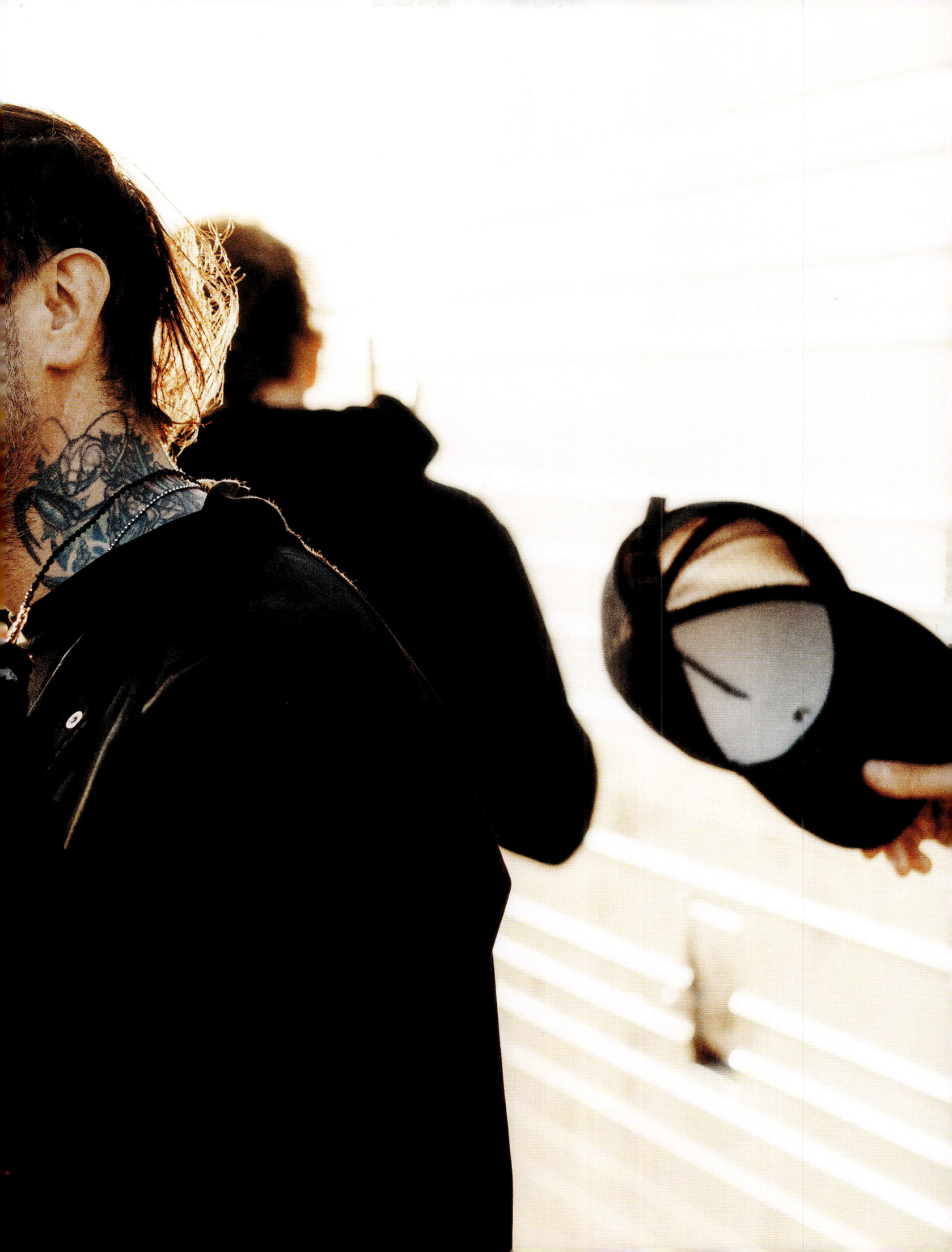

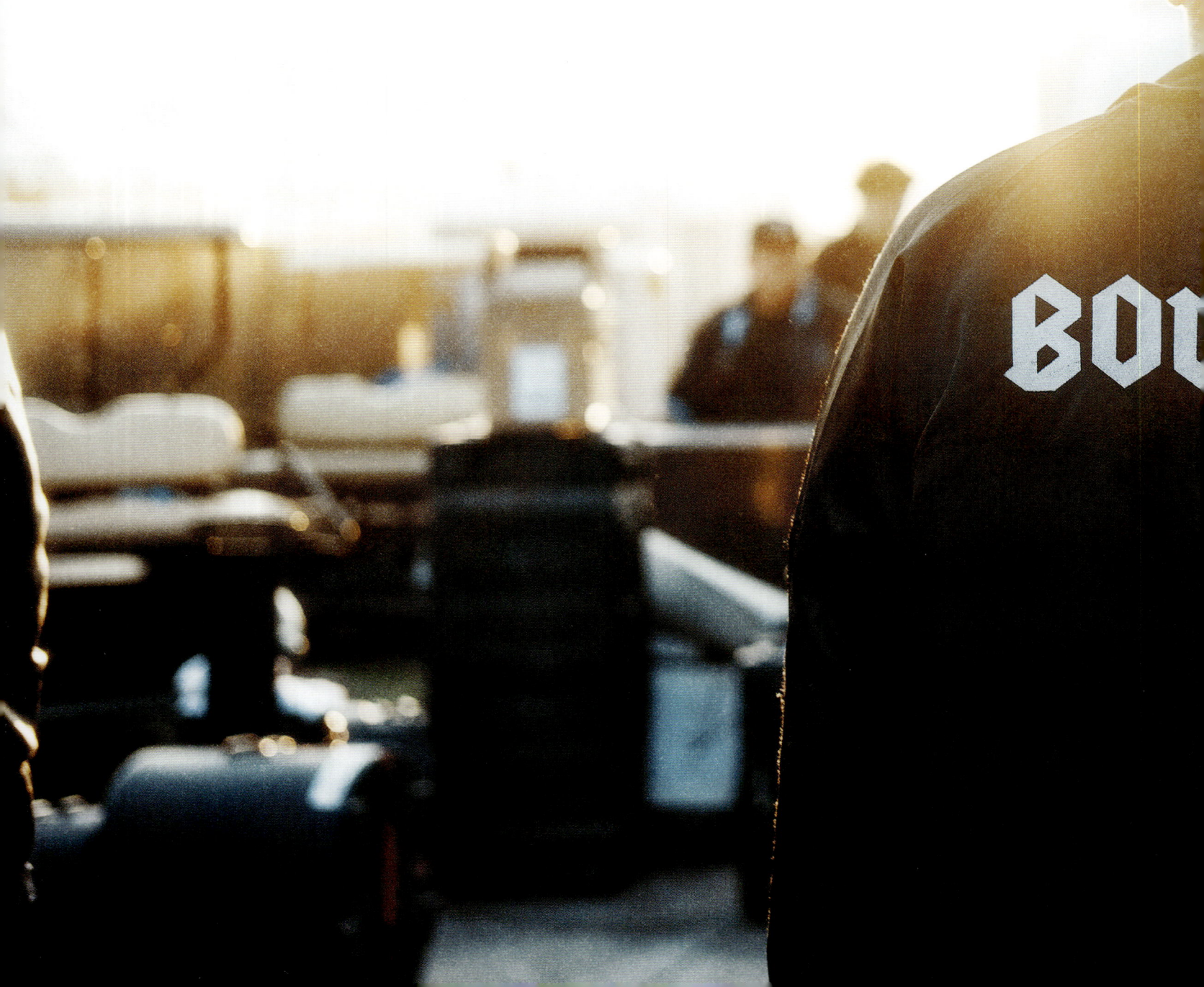

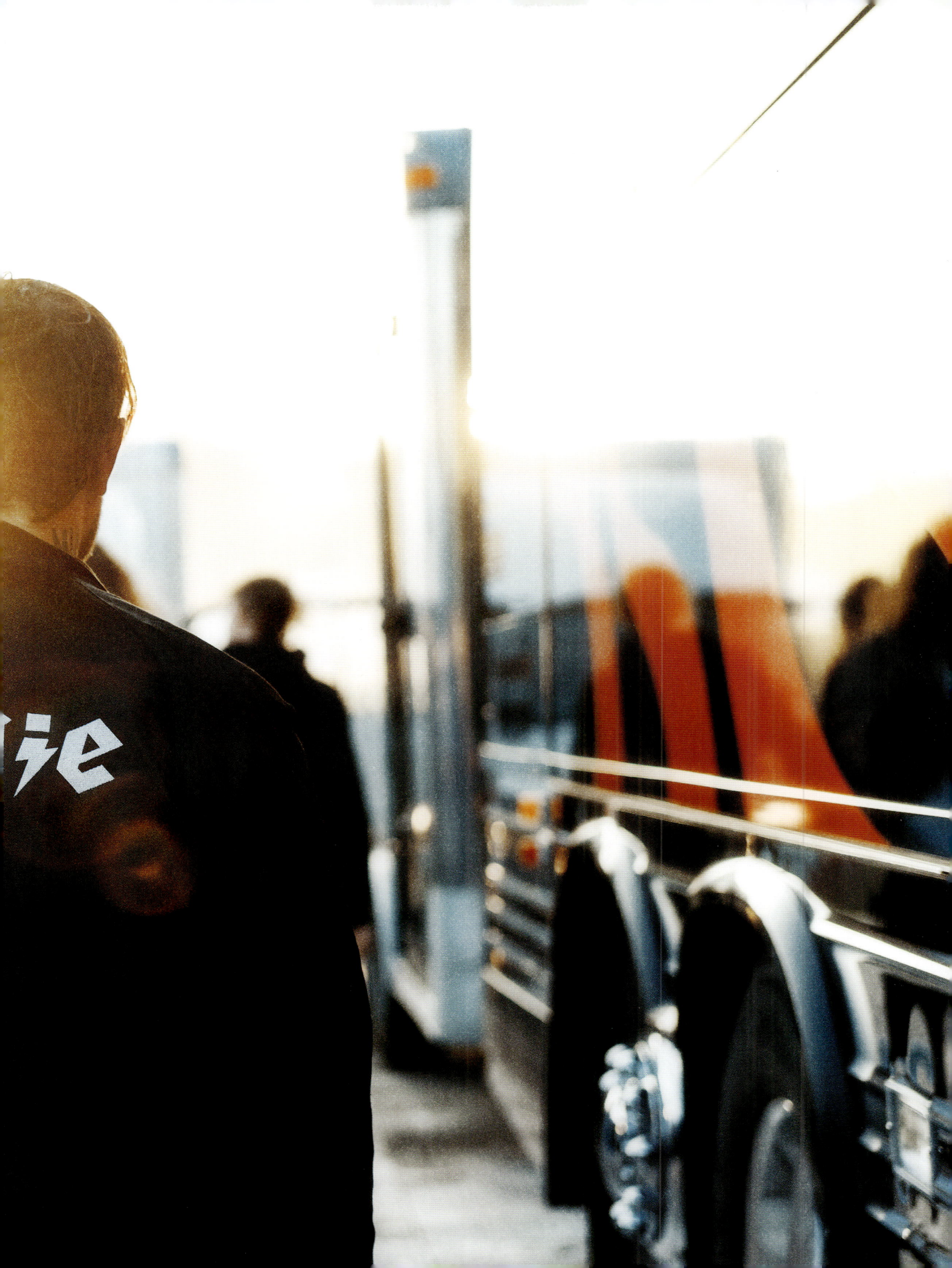

THIS IS A GENUINE RARE BIRD BOOK

Rare Bird Books
6044 North Figueroa Street
Los Angeles, California 90042
United States of America
rarebirdbooks.com

For more information, address:
Rare Bird Books Subsidiary Rights Department
6044 North Figueroa Street
Los Angeles, California 90042
United States of America

Photographs by Ryan Muirhead, Sean Akhaven, and Hunter Garrett
Additional text by Ryan J. Downey

Printed in China

10 9 8 7 6 5 4 3 2 1

Library of Congress Cataloging-in-Publication Data available upon request